Lonely Less

Lonely Less

How to Connect with Others, Make Friends and Feel Less Lonely

Gill Hasson

CAPSTONE
A Wiley Brand

This edition first published 2021
© 2021 by Gill Hasson

Registered office
John Wiley & Sons Ltd, The Atrium, Southern Gate, Chichester, West Sussex, PO19 8SQ, United Kingdom

For details of our global editorial offices, for customer services and for information about how to apply for permission to reuse the copyright material in this book please see our website at www.wiley.com.

Library of Congress Cataloging-in-Publication Data

Names: Hasson, Gill, author. | John Wiley & Sons, publisher.
Title: Lonely less : how to connect with others, make friends and feel less lonely / Gill Hasson.
Description: [Hoboken, NJ] : Wiley, 2021. | Includes index.
Identifiers: LCCN 2021017320 (print) | LCCN 2021017321 (ebook) | ISBN 9780857089045 (paperback) | ISBN 9780857089038 (adobe pdf) | ISBN 9780857089076 (epub)
Subjects: LCSH: Loneliness—Psychological aspects. | Interpersonal relations.
Classification: LCC BF575.L7 H444 2021 (print) | LCC BF575.L7 (ebook) | DDC 158.2—dc23
LC record available at https://lccn.loc.gov/2021017320
LC ebook record available at https://lccn.loc.gov/2021017321

Cover Design: Wiley

Set in 12/15pt, SabonLTStd by Straive, Chennai, India.
Printed and bound by CPI Group (UK) Ltd, Croydon, CR0 4YY

C9780857089045_180521

Being lonely goes right to the core of our wellbeing. When we're lonely we describe it with words like 'lost', 'helpless' and 'abandoned'. There is no one solution to loneliness but understanding and thinking about ways in which we can either be less lonely ourselves or help those around us is an important part of the puzzle.

Robin Hewings, Programme Director of
Campaign to End Loneliness

Loneliness is an emotion we are all likely to experience at some point in our lives. It's so important and encouraging to see the conversation normalised around it.

Amy Perrin, Founder, Marmalade Trust

Contents

Introduction

> Your life does not get better by chance. It gets better by change.
>
> Jim Rohn

Are you lonely? If so, you're not alone. Anyone – whatever their age, gender, culture, abilities, or state of health – can find themselves alone, isolated, separate in some way from others and feeling lonely.

If you *feel* lonely you *are* lonely. And it's not nice. At best, loneliness is uncomfortable. At worst, it's miserable and can leave you feeling desperate.

Human beings are social beings; we need to interact with others – to connect in positive ways and to feel that we are understood, that we belong and are valued by others. If you're lonely, there's nothing wrong with you; they might feel uncomfortable, but the lonely feelings are there to prompt you to connect with other people.

So many studies have shown that friendships boost our happiness. In 2002, Professors Ed Diener and Martin Seligman conducted a study at the University of Illinois which showed that a person's happiness is highly correlated with social relationships. They reported that 'the most salient characteristics shared by the 10% of students with the highest levels of happiness and the fewest signs of depression were their strong ties to friends and family and commitment to spending time with them'.

But what exactly *is* loneliness? How and why can a person become lonely? Chapter 1 explains this. It explains the circumstances that any one of us can find ourselves in and that result in being alone and feeling lonely.

There's no doubt that your situation – a gradual or sudden change in your circumstances – can have a direct impact on the extent to which you feel connected to others. But it's not just your circumstances – where you live, for example, or the level of access to services and social activities, or perhaps health issues, work or care commitments, or a bereavement – that can be the reason behind your loneliness. Your thoughts about your situation have a huge influence on how lonely you feel. If, for example, you get stuck thinking how unfair your situation is, believing that your loneliness is due to circumstances that you have little or no control over, then you're unlikely to be motivated to do something about it.

The problem is that feelings of loneliness can set off a downward spiral of negative thoughts and feelings which then lead to even more intense feelings of loneliness and these can serve to shut you down and close you off from others. However, the good news is that the downward spiral of negative thoughts also works in reverse: changing the way you think can lead to a change in feelings and behaviours which then generates an upward spiral *out* of loneliness

Your situation *can* change for the better!

Chapter 2 encourages you to think first about what you need and want in the way of connections and friendships. Chapter 3 then explains how you can step away from negative ways of thinking and commit yourself to more helpful ways of thinking about your situation so that you're in a better position to take positive action.

A study in 2016 by the Red Cross, in partnership with the Co-Op, discovered that 7% of those who are regularly lonely don't know where to turn for support, with many feeling there is a stigma attached to admitting feelings of loneliness, which makes it hard for them to seek help.

But there is support out there. There are people who are open to meeting others and making friends. You've just got to find them. Chapter 4 explains where to find them. It will take some time and effort on your part; you'll need to be willing to meet others, to be yourself and give something of yourself.

You might be anxious about taking the first steps towards reaching out and joining in with others, but in this chapter, as in the rest of this book, I encourage you to focus on the positive, to remind yourself what it is that you want: to connect with and get to know other people. People that you like and who like you. Focusing on the positive can give you the motivation and courage you need to take the necessary first step.

So far, so good. But once you've connected with other people, how do you turn those new connections into friendships? Again, it takes time and effort. You can't just wait for others to invite you to do things. You have to be willing to be the one to suggest doing something together. Chapter 5 has lots of ideas and advice. There are also ideas for how to maintain connections if you can't get together physically with other people.

By gathering up a bit of courage and taking those first few steps, new people and acquaintances can become friends. What if you don't have the confidence to chat easily to new people? You don't have to impress, you just have to be nice. Smile, ask questions, listen, take a genuine interest in the other person and say something about yourself. Chapter 6 has lots of advice and encouragement for you.

As you will have realized by now, to meet people, to get to know someone better and become friends, you have to reach out. But you also have to be prepared to risk rejection. If someone doesn't seem that keen on becoming friends with you, that's OK. They've got stuff going on and you don't know what it is. It's not you!

What to do though if, in a particular situation or a variety of situations, it doesn't matter what you say or do, you just don't feel like you fit in?

It's important to know that fitting in and feeling that you belong doesn't just come from being accepted by others. It starts with accepting and being yourself. It's easy to be too concerned with what others think of you, with the result that you try to be someone you're not. Rather than act like you're someone else, you need to do quite the opposite. You need to act yourself. Chapter 7 explains how to do this.

Chapter 8 moves on to looking at how you might get closer to others; to have warm, supportive friendships. It explains that you'll need to be prepared to open up yourself and be open to others. You don't have to reveal your deepest hopes, thoughts, and fears but you do need to share something that's a bit more personal than your thoughts on the weather and the price of fish! You'll also need to ask people about themselves; be interested in what they feel and think about things.

However, you'll need to be careful not to misunderstand or misinterpret the attention of others and make yourself vulnerable to others whose motives are not genuine and sincere; people who aren't good for you. Chapter 8 also explains more about this and how a difficult, negative relationship can leave you feeling isolated and lonely. You need positive people! People who you can be yourself with, who make you feel good about yourself; who listen to you and encourage you.

If you've experienced a trauma – a situation that you're currently going though or something that happened in the past – you absolutely need positive, supportive people. Unfortunately, you can feel entirely disconnected from other people as a result of a traumatic experience. Even if you do have good friends and family members, you may feel that no one understands. As a result, you might withdraw from others; you might find it difficult to relate to or trust others.

Whatever trauma you've experienced there will be support there for you. Professional help and/or a support group that can provide a safe place to share, be listened to, get advice, support, and information. You can connect with others via phone, video, email, or in person. You've just got to make the first move and be persistent in finding the support that's right for you. Chapter 9 and the Further Information pages at the back of the book can be of help.

Chapter 10 moves on to time spent alone. Of course relationships are important but they're not the only way to feel connected. We each need to balance time with others and time on our own. You need to feel at ease without others; to be comfortable and enjoy some time alone. Instead of getting stuck in feelings of loneliness, your mind is better placed looking for ways to make time on your own easier. How can you make time alone easier? By doing things that you enjoy and make you feel good. Chapter 10 has plenty of ideas and suggestions.

Chapter 11 turns to the subject of loneliness at work. It recognizes that it's not just working from home that can be isolating and lonely; working with others amongst difficult, unsupportive relationships can leave you feeling isolated and lonely too. Again, there's advice and suggestions in this chapter too.

Finally, Chapter 12 has advice for reaching out to others who may also be struggling with feelings of loneliness. Whether they want to connect with others and take part in social activities, find people to make friends with, feel less isolated at work, or they have particular difficulty or have experienced a trauma, your concern, kindness, and support can make a big difference. In fact, if you'd like to make a sustained difference on a regular basis in helping others to feel less lonely, there's a range of global, national, and local initiatives and organizations you can sign up to.

Whether you want to be less lonely, connect with others, make friends and feel that you belong or you want to help others to be the same, as the saying goes – it's never too late to be what you want to be!

1
Understanding Loneliness

All the lonely people
Where do they all come from?
All the lonely people
Where do they all belong?

Lennon and McCartney

Defining Loneliness

There's a difference between being alone and being lonely. To be alone simply means to be separate, to be apart in some way. You could be physically alone, for example – the only person in the room. Or, in another example, amongst a group of other people, you might be alone in your thoughts and feelings, opinions, and beliefs about something.

The crucial difference between being alone and being lonely concerns how you feel about being alone. If you're not OK with being on your own in a particular situation, you'll feel lonely. But if you *are* OK – if you feel quite comfortable – being alone in that situation won't be a difficulty for you.

In fact, there are times when you might choose to be alone; you may have chosen solitude. Solitude is being alone by choice; it's wanting to be alone and being comfortable in your own company. In contrast, loneliness is unwanted – it's not wanting to be alone. Solitude is something you might seek. Loneliness is something you probably want to avoid.

The difference between solitude and loneliness could be described as the difference between, for example, enjoying watching a film or box set on your own, versus crying on the sofa because you wish you had someone to watch that film or box set with.

If you are lonely, you're probably feeling you are without friendly companionship and support; that you are not connected in a meaningful way to others, to the world, to life. You may well feel that no one understands you or that they misunderstand you.

At its best, loneliness is uncomfortable and at its worst, it's downright miserable and can leave you feeling wretched, depressed, even despairing. Loneliness can leave you questioning your value to others and where in life you belong.

The Purpose of Loneliness

But if being lonely leaves us feeling sad and unhappy, why do we experience it? What possible purpose can the loneliness serve?

As the first few lines of Benjamin Zephaniah's poem 'People Need People' tell us:

People need people,

To walk to

To talk to

To cry and rely on,

People will always need people.

To love and to miss

To hug and to kiss

It's true; people *do* need people. Human beings are social beings; we need to interact with others; to connect in positive ways and to feel that we belong and are valued. People need people to look out for each other's well-being and to keep each other safe, both physically and mentally.

Loneliness serves a purpose in the same way that hunger and thirst serve a purpose. Hunger and thirst send signals; those signals are uncomfortable *physical* feelings that prompt you to eat and drink. Loneliness also sends a signal; it's an uncomfortable *emotional* feeling that alerts you to the fact that you need to connect to others.

Knowing that feelings of loneliness are a part of the human condition can reassure you that, if you're lonely, there's nothing wrong with you – you're simply experiencing feelings that are a natural prompt for you to do something about it; to connect with other people.

We are like islands in the sea, separate on the surface but connected in the deep.

William James

How do you know if you are lonely?

Loneliness is subjective. No matter how many or how few people you are connected to, no matter how many friends you have, no matter how well you get on or how well you fit in with others, if you *feel* lonely, you *are* lonely.

Loneliness may be an occasional, passing feeling that you can manage or it may be more long term. You might feel a bit lonely or you might feel very lonely or feel somewhere in between.

Different Ways of Being Lonely

There is, though, more than one way of experiencing loneliness; you might be socially lonely and/or emotionally lonely and/or experiencing existential loneliness.

Social loneliness happens when you have very few or no friends, family, or community; you have little or no contact with others and are unhappy about it.

Emotional loneliness happens when you feel that you are missing a close meaningful relationship or relationships. You may have one or more friends, colleagues, family, and/or a partner, but with some or all of those people, you don't feel close – you don't feel that you have a shared warmth, understanding, and empathy.

You might become aware of being emotionally lonely if you need someone to talk to about something going on in your life, but feel that there is no one – or not the right person or people – who would be interested or care to talk with you.

You might, for example, have a particular perspective, belief, opinion, or feeling about something that no one around you shares or agrees with. If it bothers you that you're alone with your beliefs – that no one shares your perspective, opinions, or feelings – you may feel unhappy that you're not understood or that you're misunderstood. You might feel that you don't fit in; that you don't belong.

No doubt you've heard the cliché that it's possible to feel lonely in a crowd. You've probably also heard the saying 'Hell is other people'. Well, loneliness, like hell, can be other people.

Loneliness isn't [just] the physical absence of other people ... it's the sense that you're not sharing anything that matters with anyone else. If you have lots of people around you .... but you don't share anything that matters with them, then you'll still be lonely.

Johann Hari

As well as social and emotional loneliness, another type of loneliness is existential loneliness. Existential loneliness happens if you're feeling entirely separate and disconnected from other people as a result of a challenging, difficult, or traumatic experience. It could be a situation that you're currently going though or something that happened in the past. Whatever the issue and the circumstances, experiencing a trauma can leave you feeling, amongst other things, disconnected; lonely, anxious, and vulnerable.

Each state of loneliness – social, emotional, and existential loneliness – can overlap with another; it wouldn't be unusual to experience one or more types of loneliness at the same time. You might, for example, feel socially lonely *and* emotionally lonely – that you have few, if any, friends and that with the people you do know, you don't feel close to any of them.

Why Might You Feel Lonely? The External Circumstances that Can cause Loneliness

Whether you are experiencing social, emotional, or spiritual loneliness, for however long a period and however intensely you feel lonely, you're not alone. Research published in 2016 by the Co-Op in partnership with the British Red Cross estimated that, one way or another, loneliness affects 9 million people across the UK.

The causes of loneliness are varied. They include issues to do with your external circumstances – where you live, for example – and your internal circumstances – your mindset; the way you think about your situation.

If you're lonely it could be that you:

- Live on your own; you have little in the way of companionship.
- Live in an isolated part of the country; there's little in the way of social activities to join in with and limited services such as public transport. Maybe you don't have your own transport.
- Have little or no money to join in with the activities you'd like to be involved in.
- Have a physical disability or illness; you might find it difficult to get out and about.
- Have a cognitive disability or a mental health problem which makes it difficult to communicate and connect with others.
- Work or have other commitments such as family and care responsibilities that leave you with little or no free time for a social life.
- Don't feel that you fit in at your place of work, university, college, or school.
- Work from home and feel isolated from your workplace and colleagues.
- Belong to a minority group and live in an area without others from a similar background.
- Have been excluded by others because of, for example, your gender or sexual orientation; your family situation; or your age, culture, or religion.
- Have experienced discrimination, abuse, or trauma of some kind which has left you feeling isolated.

Circumstances that lead to loneliness may happen gradually – a deteriorating health condition, whether your own or your partner's – or it may be triggered by a particular event.

Although moving to a new area – a new country or culture for example – or starting university, beginning a new job, or becoming a parent can be exciting and positive, people often find that new experiences or a change in their situation or circumstances can make initiating and developing friendships difficult.

Starting University

Going from growing up in a place where I had family and friends and knew lots of people, to being plonked into a university campus on the outskirts of a big city was a bewildering, lonely time for me. Removed from my family and friends, trying to work out who I was and where and how I fitted in was a struggle.

I'd watch out of my room, everyone else going out in the evenings and at the weekends. (I later found out it wasn't everyone else, many other students had been in their rooms feeling as lonely and unhappy as I was.) I retreated into myself and spent a lot of time in my tiny room in the university's halls of residence, talking on the phone to my sister and best friend back home. It took time for me to get to know others and make friends.

As well as making it difficult to make new friendships, a change in circumstances can also disconnect you from the friendships and social ties you used to have.

For example, if you're no longer working then you no longer have the same level of social contact you enjoyed at work.

The Internet, Social Media, and Loneliness

Are lonely people more attracted to the internet, or can the internet actually cause loneliness? Certainly, some people may choose to withdraw from face-to-face social interactions so they can have more time for the internet.

In 2018, 55,000 people took part in the BBC's Loneliness Experiment in collaboration with Wellcome Collection. Amongst the findings, the study showed that people who feel lonely don't use social media any more often than other people, but they use it differently. They have more Facebook friends who they are only friends with online and who don't overlap with their real-life friends.

Excessive use, especially if passive, can increase isolation. While moderate use, especially by users who engage with others rather than just passively consume content, can increase social connection, facilitate social interaction, and enable people to find the information, advice, and support they might need that will help reduce loneliness.

When it comes to engagement with social media for example, people who spend more time on these platforms tend to report greater feelings of loneliness and poorer wellbeing. But similarly, some of this is correlational, meaning that people who are lonely may just be more likely to use social media in the first place. We might know some of the short-term effects of heavy engagement with social media, but we don't yet have a really good grasp on the long-term effects of it.

Dr Holt-Lunstad, Professor of Psychology and
Neuroscience. Brigham Young University

Whatever the circumstances that have caused loneliness, the result is the same: you feel disconnected and alone and you're unhappy about it.

Why Might You Feel Lonely? Your Mindset – the Internal Circumstances – that Can Cause Loneliness

But being lonely isn't just a result of sudden or gradual change in circumstances. As well as external circumstances, there are internal circumstances; psychological and emotional aspects to loneliness; the thoughts and feelings that influence our experience of loneliness.

Is Loneliness a Mental Health Problem?

Although there are psychological and emotional aspects to loneliness, that's not to suggest that loneliness is, in itself, a mental health problem.

However, the UK mental health charity Mind says that loneliness and mental health *are* strongly linked. 'Having a mental health problem can increase your chance of feeling lonely. For example, some people may have misconceptions about what certain mental health problems mean, so you may find it difficult to speak to them about your problems.

Or you may experience social phobia – social anxiety – and find it difficult to engage in everyday activities involving other people, which could lead to a lack of meaningful social contact and cause feelings of loneliness.

Feeling lonely can also have a negative impact on your mental health, especially if these feelings have lasted a long time. Some research suggests that loneliness is associated with an increased risk of certain mental health problems, including depression, anxiety, low self-esteem, sleep problems and increased stress.'

Mindsets

Loneliness can influence how you might anticipate and interpret social situations; although you want to connect with others, you may have lost confidence and self-esteem and therefore feel apprehensive about being with other people.

It could also be that when you *are* with other people you're sensitive to whether you think others are or are not being friendly and welcoming towards you. If people don't meet your expectations – aren't as friendly and inclusive as you would like – you might withdraw further. You might, for example, be a new parent and decide to go along to a parent and baby club for the first time, or you might be an older person and decide to try out a local lunch club. If you feel that other members weren't as welcoming as you had hoped, you could easily dismiss the group and its members as being unfriendly and conclude that you don't belong there. This could then add to your feelings of low confidence and self-esteem.

If you've tried for some time to connect with people, you may feel that you have done all you can; you've made an effort to make friends and to fit in, to connect with someone who understands you, but to no avail. You feel upset and frustrated.

Frustration can lead to resentment which in turn can lead to cynicism and suspicion of other people. That frustration may surface when you're with other people which, of course, can be off-putting to others; make them less likely to want to connect with you and they pull away.

Isolation and loneliness increases our wanting to blame others for feelings of not being included, not belonging. In such situations we are vulnerable to having conversations in our head with others and coming to conclusions based on those fantasies.

Philippa Perry

It's easy for your mind to get caught up in ruminative cycles of emotions including anger, resentment, and fear as well as emptiness, sadness, disappointment, and even shame. Rather than prompting you to do something positive about it, these feelings can create a downward spiral where loneliness causes you to withdraw further.

Attributional Styles

When people feel lonely they think and act differently to when they do not feel lonely. And not always in helpful ways.

Your attributional style – how you explain/interpret the reasons you're lonely – influences what you do or don't do about it. If you believe that your loneliness is due to situations and circumstances that are permanent and unlikely to change – and that you have little or no control over – then it's unlikely you're going to be able to change your circumstances or situation. Why? Because if you have already convinced yourself that loneliness is due to situations and circumstances that you have little or no control over, you're not going to have much in the way of motivation to try and do something about it. You're not even willing to try.

The more often you tell yourself that your situation is hopeless, the more you 'learn' or 'teach' yourself that you have very little control over what happens to you, other people, situations, and events. Furthermore, having 'learned' to believe in your limitations and lack of control, you resign yourself to believing that, more often than not, you are helpless and situations are often hopeless.

Loneliness Changes Our Perceptions of the World

A 2019 study carried out at King's College London asked 2000 18-year-olds to describe the friendliness of their neighbourhood. The participants' siblings, living at the same address, were asked the same question. The lonelier siblings perceived their neighbourhoods as less friendly, less cohesive, and less trustworthy than their brother or sister who suffered less from feelings of isolation.

But although loneliness can arise from external circumstances, it absolutely does not mean that you have no control and that your situation can't change for the better.

So, What to Do?

Whether you're experiencing social, emotional, or existential loneliness or a combination of states of loneliness, there are two approaches to improving your situation.

The first approach involves exploring ways to connect with others, increase opportunities for social interaction, and/or to feel understood, valued – that you belong and that you fit in.

The second approach – which is just as important and goes hand in hand with the first – is to develop the right mindset, one that provides the constructive thoughts, feelings, and attitudes that will help you feel confident and positive that you can improve your situation and stop feeling so lonely.

The next step is to look at what loneliness feels like and what ways of thinking are helpful or unhelpful in dealing with it.

In a nutshell

- If you're alone you're separate; apart from other people in some way. If you are lonely, you are unhappy being alone.
- Solitude is being alone by choice. Loneliness is unwanted; it's not wanting to be alone. Solitude is something you might seek. Loneliness is something you probably want to avoid.
- If you *feel* lonely, you *are* lonely.
- Feelings of loneliness are a part of the human condition; the feelings that are there to prompt you to connect with other people.
- There is more than one way of experiencing loneliness; you might be socially lonely and/or emotionally lonely and/or experiencing existential loneliness.
- Loneliness happens as a result of your external circumstances – where you live, for example – and your internal circumstances; your mindset; your thoughts and feelings about your situation.

- The circumstances that lead to loneliness may happen gradually or may be triggered by a particular event.
- Loneliness can influence how you might anticipate and interpret social situations; you may have lost confidence and self-esteem.
- When you are with other people, if they aren't as friendly as you would like, you might withdraw further.
- Your mind can easily get caught up in ruminative cycles of negative emotions.
- Any frustration and resentment you show can be off-putting to others; make them less likely to want to connect with you and they pull away.
- Your attributional style – how you explain/interpret the reasons you're lonely – influences what you do or don't do about it.
- If you believe that loneliness is due to situations and circumstances that you have little or no control over, you're not going to be motivated to do something about it.
- You can do something about it; your situation can change for the better! There are two things to do: (1) Explore the many different ways to connect with others to (2) Develop a positive mindset.

2
Knowing What You Want

Friendship is the hardest thing in the world to explain. It's not something you learn in school. But if you haven't learned the meaning of friendship, you really haven't learned anything.

Muhammad Ali

Very often, people try random ways to connect with others but then lose hope and feel worse when they have little or no success. A better approach – before you do anything else – is to, first, identify the external causes and circumstances that have contributed towards you being lonely and, secondly, to think through what you want in the way of connections and friendships. If you start by doing this, you are in a better position to focus your efforts and more likely to find the right solutions; solutions that work for *you*.

Why, then, are you lonely? What could be the reason? Turn back to page 9 and read through the examples of external causes of loneliness. Do any of those situations reflect your situation or do you think you're lonely for another reason?

Do you think that loneliness crept up on you or has it been triggered by a particular event?

Are there particular circumstances or situations that leave you feeling lonely? Are there times of the week or the day when you feel more lonely than other times? The weekends or evenings perhaps?

Next, you need to be clear about what it is you want in the way of connections and friendships with other people. What's important to you in a friendship and in your relationships with others?

Perhaps you are socially lonely and you simply want some companionship – someone or some people to just be there – a physical presence – to chat with about what was on TV last night, the weather, the state of the world, sports, or celebrity gossip.

I have plenty of people to do things with, I just have no one to do nothing with.

Felicity Green

Do you want one or more friends to hang out with – to do fun, interesting things together; go to gigs, learn a new skill, maybe have weekend away or a holiday together? Certainly having shared interests or shared experiences creates connections and bonds between people. But while sharing the same interests – a love of hip-hop music or a passion for football for example – might be important to some people in a friendship, it could be that for you, mutual support, care, and concern are more important aspects of a friendship. It could be that you are emotionally lonely. You may or may not have other people in your life but the problem is that you don't feel close to them, you don't feel that you have a meaningful connection to anyone.

Perhaps you don't feel like you fit in or belong – that, for whatever reason, no one 'gets' you. Do you want someone or a few people you can feel close to and with whom you can share confidences and the events in your life? Would you like someone or some others who understand you and get where you're coming from; that you share a mutual empathy with and can turn to when you need help, support, and encouragement?

Maybe you want to be part of a group or community where you feel included and involved – that you are valued, respected, and that you belong?

It could be that you've experienced or are currently experiencing some difficulties and challenges in your life. If something traumatic has happened to you and you're experiencing existential loneliness, feeling entirely separate from other people – do you need understanding and support for what you've been through or are currently going through?

Be aware that no one person can meet all your social and emotional needs and give you everything you might want from a friendship. Different people have their different abilities and strengths. One person might be a good listener, but you can't rely on them to be there when you need them. Someone else may be loyal, but you don't have much in common. Someone else might help you out at the drop of a hat, but they're not much fun. And so on.

How Many Friends Do You Need?

> We have three types of friends in life: Friends for a reason, friends for a season and friends for a lifetime.
>
> Author unknown

More than two thousand years ago, the Greek philosopher Aristotle identified three different kinds of friendship:

- friendships of utility,
- friendships of pleasure,
- friendships of virtue.

With 'friendships of utility', the relationship is one of mutual benefit; one way or another, it's useful to both you and the other person. That person could be a colleague, customer, or client or, for example, a neighbour with whom you exchange each other's gardening or household tools, feed the cat, and check each other's houses when you go on holiday.

Aristotle's 'friendships of pleasure' are friendships that exist between you and those with whom you enjoy a shared interest: people who support the same team or play in the same sports team as you, a book club, choir, dance class, etc.

Both types of friendship usually end when circumstances change; when a friendship of utility is no longer beneficial to one or both of you; one of you leaves the job, or the neighbour moves away. Friendships of pleasure also often end when what you have in common comes to an end: when one or both of you leave the team, the club, the course you were both attending.

Whether it's friendships of utility and/or friendships of pleasure, if you feel you have few or none of these types of relationship, you're likely to feel socially lonely.

The third type of friendship that Aristotle identified are what he called 'friendships of virtue', which are based on mutual respect and admiration. These friendships may take more time to establish than the other two kinds, but they're also stronger and more enduring. They often arise between you and someone else who has similar values and goals to you; you have similar ideas about your lives and how the world should be.

Aristotle pointed out that there can't be a large number of friends in a virtuous friendship group because the amount of time and care that this type of friendship needs limits the amount of time you can spend with other friends.

Fast forward to the 21st century and Aristotle's theory still holds true. Anthropologist and evolutionary biologist Professor Robin Dunbar agrees that there's a limit to the number of friendships that any one person can have.

Professor Dunbar suggests that we maintain a series of social networks. In the first circle are people you know through work or a leisure interest. They are the people you might invite to a big party but with whom your relationship never turns into anything deeper. Most relationships in this group have a natural life cycle. Often we're drawn together by circumstance – work, the single life, children – and, as Aristotle noted, as our situations change we tend to go our separate ways.

The next group are the people you would call friends. You might see them often, but not so much that you consider them to be true intimates. Then there's the circle of 15: the good friends that you can turn to for a degree of support when you need it. People move in and out of these different friendship groups and sometimes fall out of them altogether.

The most intimate relationships in 'Dunbar's number' – five – would be those a person could consider as their close friends and may include family members. Some people have more than three close friends and some have fewer. It's these friendships and relationships that provide the emotional support we need.

Whatever the causes or reasons for being lonely, whatever you're looking for in the way of connections and friendships with other people, once you're clearer about those causes and reasons, and what you want in the way of relationships, you can focus more clearly on your efforts.

In a nutshell

- By identifying the reasons – the external and the internal circumstances – that have contributed towards your loneliness and thinking about what you want in the way of connections and friendships, you're in a better position to focus your efforts and be more likely to find the right solutions; solutions that work for *you*.

3
Positive Thinking

The longest relationship you will ever have is with your-self. So would you like to take your self-critic with you, or your compassionate friend?

Deborah Lee

One of the key problems with feeling lonely is that feelings of loneliness can set off a downward spiral of negative thoughts and feelings which then leads to even more intense feelings of loneliness. In turn, these thoughts and feelings influence what you do and don't do. Too often, instead of prompting you to do something positive to connect with other people you may do just the opposite: withdraw from possible contact and con-nection with others. And that just makes it even harder to take positive steps towards connecting and making friends.

Negative ways of thinking – often referred to as 'cog-nitive distortions' – can make you feel bad about the world, other people, yourself and your abilities, and limit the opportunities and possibilities that could change your situation for the better.

There are a number of ways that negative thoughts occur. Here are some examples:

Confirmation bias. Confirmation bias involves consciously or unconsciously looking for evidence to support and confirm what you've already decided is true, while avoiding or ignoring contradictory information. For example, you invite someone to do something with you – go to the cinema, for example – but they decline. The next person you invite also declines and gives a weak excuse (or at least, *you* perceive it as a weak excuse) as to why they can't join you. You interpret this as proof that there's something unlikeable about you; that no one wants to do things with you. But you forget or ignore the occasions in the past when others *have* accepted your invitations to events or outings.

Jumping to conclusions. This involves judging or deciding something without having all the relevant information. You anticipate that things will turn out badly. For example, you think 'I could go to that drop-in/sign up for that activity/ join that club ...' but you immediately follow that idea with '... but there won't be anyone of interest to me/won't be anyone who wants to talk to me.' You've reacted to a positive thought with a negative conclusion.

Mind reading. With mind reading, you believe you know what the other person is thinking and that their thoughts and intentions are negative. For example, 'they'll think I'm boring. They're probably wondering why I'm even here.'

Polarized thinking. Polarized thinking is 'all or nothing' thinking. With polarized thinking, there's no middle ground and no grey areas. Polarized thinking is often characterized by terms such as 'should' or 'shouldn't'; 'must' or 'mustn't'; 'every', 'always', or 'never'. For example, 'They *must* know I'm on my own – they *should* know I'm lonely.' Or, in another example, 'There's *absolutely no point* trying to explain how I feel. It won't make *any* difference. *No one* will *ever* understand.'

Blaming. This involves placing all responsibility for being lonely on someone or something else. You see yourself as helpless; a victim of other people or external factors. Perhaps you blame yourself: 'I'm lonely because I'm old/have a disability/ I'm different to other people.' You might, for example, say things to yourself such as: 'I'm never going to fit in. I always seem to say the wrong thing.'

You might blame others: 'People never invite me to do things with them' or where you live: 'I live in the middle of nowhere. Nothing ever happens round here.'

Your negative interpretations of yourself and other people, situations, and circumstances undermine your confidence and/or leave you feeling frustrated and resentful.

Comparing. This happens when you compare what you think is the worst of yourself and your situation with the best you presume about others. You may think other people are better or have it better than you: better skills, abilities, or personal qualities and better or more resources. For example, you might think, 'It's not fair, his family visit him much more than mine do.'

You might also compare your current situation with past circumstances; you look back on other times and circumstances in your life and feel that everything was so much better then. You had friends and people to spend time and share interests with. You were happy.

Why Negative Thinking Is Unhelpful

Negative thoughts and cognitive distortions – blaming, comparing, mindreading, jumping to conclusions, etc. – will convince you that you have little or no control over your circumstances.

No doubt you believe that what you think is true. Maybe it *is* true. Maybe, for example, if you join that club, you *won't* find anyone that you click with. Perhaps your limited physical mobility or communication *is* a barrier to getting out and about as much as you'd like. It could be that everyone at your new job knows each other well and it *is* going to take time to get accepted and feel that you belong. Perhaps you *were* less lonely and happier in the past. But for all these difficulties, there *are* solutions!

It's really important that you understand that once you get stuck in negative thoughts they can trigger further limiting, unhelpful thoughts and reactions which just serve to shut you down and close you off from others.

Repeated negative ways of thinking can lead to a concept known as 'learned helplessness'. This means that, in effect, you 'learn' or 'teach' yourself that you have little or no control over what happens to you, other people, situations, and events. You convince yourself there's no way out of problems and difficulties; there's nothing you can do to change things.

While it's important not to deny or suppress how you feel – you do need to acknowledge your hurt and sadness – getting stuck in self-pity, frustration and resentment not only creates pain for you but can alienate others; they avoid you because they feel uncomfortable around you. You may then see that as something else to feel hurt about (confirmation bias) rather than see the pain you are creating for yourself.

However, the good news is that the downward spiral of negative thoughts and despair, leading to more intense feelings of loneliness, also works in reverse: changing the way you think can lead to a change in feelings and behaviours which then generates an upward spiral *out* of loneliness.

Recognize Negative Self Talk

Because the way you think is habitual, you probably don't even recognize the nature of your thoughts and reactions to events. In fact, your negative thoughts are so powerful *because* you rarely have conscious awareness or control over them. You simply accept what you're thinking and respond accordingly.

The first step, then, in managing negative thinking is simply to become more aware of it; to identify the way you think and explain things to yourself.

Top Tip

Use your feelings to alert you to how you are thinking: whenever you're feeling lonely – feeling upset or frustrated and resentful – write down your thoughts. Write down how you're feeling and what you're thinking. Do this – write down your thoughts and feelings – for a week or two, either in a notebook or on your phone.

As well as being more aware of individual negative thoughts, you may notice a pattern or theme emerging. You may realize that you're inclined to jump to conclusions or that you get caught up in blaming or negative comparisons. You may notice too what sort of circumstances trigger your negative thoughts.

When you become aware that you're thinking negatively about yourself, other people, and the world, see those thoughts as a signal – a red flag – that's letting you know your thoughts are unhelpful. The function of those thoughts can then change, rather than dragging you down, you can regard them as a cue for more helpful, positive thinking.

Turn your face to the sun and the shadows fall behind you.

Maori proverb

Ask yourself: 'In what way does thinking like this help me feel better about myself, my situation, and other people?' When you ask yourself 'Is this thought helpful?' you're not disputing the accuracy of your thoughts – maybe, for example, the other person *won't* accept your invitation to do something with you, maybe there *isn't* anyone who really understands you, but right now, regardless of their accuracy, getting stuck in these thoughts isn't helping you. They're preventing you from coming up with any solutions.

Top Tips

- Refuse to get stuck and wallow in negative thoughts. Simply say 'Stop!' to yourself. Or 'No, I'm not going there. I'm not thinking like that!' Or, try using a thought-changing prompt; if you're sitting down, stand up. If you're standing up, sit down. If you're indoors, go to a different room. If you're out walking, cross to the other side of the road or change the direction you're walking.

- Think about what you would say to someone else in the same situation to make them feel better. What kind, helpful things would you say to a friend? How would you reassure them? What would you suggest they do? Now do that for yourself.

Moving on to Positive Thoughts and Actions: Acceptance and Commitment

There's a concept in the practice of mindfulness – 'Acceptance and Commitment' – that can help you let go of unhelpful thoughts and move on to helpful thoughts. An acceptance and commitment approach suggests that you don't challenge your negative thoughts. Instead, you simply notice and accept that you are thinking negatively about your situation. Then you step back from those thoughts, let them go, and move on to more helpful ways of thinking, responding, and behaving.

Acceptance and commitment recognizes that when you accept and let go of negative unhelpful thoughts, you let go of the emotional aspects and allow the rational, logical part of your mind to start working for you; to think in more helpful, positive ways.

Supposing, for example, your thoughts about something were: 'Everyone at my new job/class/club/community has been there for ages; they know each other well, it's going to take ages for me to be accepted and feel that I belong.' Whether your thinking is correct or not – it may or may not take ages to feel part of the new group – you simply acknowledge and accept that it's not helping you to get stuck in thinking like this and you move on to thinking – to committing yourself to – more helpful thoughts and solutions. So, in this example, you'd accept that maybe it is going to take time and effort to get to feel like you belong; then you'd move on from there and commit yourself to thinking about what you can do now – in the present – to move forward.

An acceptance and commitment approach is a mindful approach because it emphasizes that no matter what you thought before, what matters is how you think and what you do from now on. The focus is on positive, helpful ways of thinking and behaving.

Top Tip

Any time you catch yourself saying a negative sentence about feeling lonely, add the word 'but'. The word 'but' will prompt you to follow up with a positive sentence. Here's an example:

> I don't have anyone I can talk to about how I feel *but* I can find out about a relevant helpline or support group and talk to someone who will listen and understand.

How could you finish this sentence?

'As a full time carer I don't have any time to meet other people. But ...

Looking Forward

There's nothing wrong with reminiscing – looking back on good times in your life – but dwelling on those times can keep you stuck and deceive you into thinking you can't ever be that happy again. Instead, nostalgia can be used as a stepping stone towards improving your situation: knowing you made connections and had friends in the past can reassure you that you *can* initiate and develop friendships again.

When my grandparents moved after 50 years of living in a town in Kent to live near us in Sussex, I was concerned. I asked my grandmother: 'Is moving a good idea? What about the friends and community you've known for so long; won't you miss them?' She simply replied: 'We've made friends before. We can make friends again.' And of course, with that attitude, they did.

In a nutshell

- Feelings of loneliness can set off a downward spiral of negative thoughts and feelings which then leads to even more intense feelings of loneliness.
- If you get stuck in negative thoughts they can trigger further limiting, unhelpful thoughts and reactions which just serve to shut you down and close you off from others.
- The good news is that the downward spiral of negative thoughts and despair, leading to more intense feelings of loneliness, also works in reverse: changing the way you think can lead to a change in feelings and behaviours which then generates an upward spiral *out* of loneliness.
- The first step in managing negative thinking is simply to become more aware of it; to identify the way you think and explain things to yourself.
- An acceptance and commitment approach suggests that you don't challenge your negative thoughts. Instead, you simply notice and accept that you are thinking negatively about your situation. Then you step away from those thoughts and commit yourself to more helpful ways of thinking, responding, and behaving.

4
Meeting New People

A friend may be waiting behind a stranger's face.

Maya Angelou

After she became unemployed and her closest friends moved away, Jessica Pan, author of *Sorry I'm Late, I Didn't Want to Come: An Introvert's Year of Living Dangerously*, reflected on what she wanted from life. What she wanted, she realized, was 'some new friends who I felt truly connected to and more confidence. Was that too much to ask? Surely not. So what were other people with ... close friends and rich fulfilling lives doing that I wasn't? Eventually and with mounting fear, I realised: they were having new experiences, taking risks, making new connections. They were actually out there, living in the world instead of staring out at it.'

If, like Jessica, you want to connect with others and make new friends, the good news is that there *are* people who are open to meeting others and making friends too. You've just got to find them. Those people are unlikely to come knocking on the door, it takes effort on your part; you need to be willing to meet others, to be yourself and give something of yourself. You *can* make new friends but, as Jessica recognized, you have to get out there.

We want to encourage people to see loneliness as a blank canvas on which they can fill their lives with new friends and experiences.

www.marmaladetrust.org

But where to start? A good way forward is to start with your interests. When you have interests and activities you enjoy, you can meet and join in with people who have similar interests. Whether it's playing or watching a sport, a creative activity, or an enjoyment of arts and culture, getting together with people who like and enjoy the same things as you makes it easier for you to talk to them and make friends because you've already got something in common; you share similar interests and values.

Have a look at www.meetup.com. Their website enables people to find and join groups of other people in their local area who share each other's interests. There are Meetup groups to fit a wide range of interests and hobbies, plus others you'll never have thought of. There are book groups, art groups, film and theatre groups, and sci-fi groups. Hiking and running groups, football groups, netball groups, and cycling groups. There are groups centred round particular age groups, cultures, and identities: '20s–30s' and '40s–60s' groups, for example; Japanese appreciation groups, conservation groups, singles groups, LGBTQ groups and so on. (You can also start your own new Meetup group.)

People who go to 'Meetups' do so knowing they'll be meeting people who are also open to meeting other people with a shared interest or identity and making new friends. If you find people who are just as keen on, for example, board games, Nordic walking, or craft beers as you are, then you'll find it relatively easy to connect and make friends with them. And when you're doing something that's fun and meaningful, your ability to form connections will come naturally. It's a win-win situation – you get to do something you enjoy and you also have the opportunity to meet new people.

You'll most likely get a sense of what the group is like from the first meeting, so the most important step is to show up and see what it's like. If, in the first few meetings, you do meet one or two people you like, because they'll likely be at the next meeting and the one after that, it means you can let a friendship develop naturally, over time.

With any group, there are usually new members joining, so as well as the regulars, there's the potential to meet more people over the coming months.

Don't hesitate to contact the organizer first if you have any questions; you might want to know more about the group: how many people usually attend; the age range, gender, or cultural mix; accessibility and parking, etc.

47

Trying Something New

As well as a current interest or hobby, you could try something new. Have you, for example, ever wanted to learn how to speak Spanish, to dance the tango? What about paddle boarding or cold water swimming? Perhaps you'd like to take up photography, Mexican cooking, or quilting. Why not take the plunge and try a new activity?

Take a Class

You can search for courses by going to your local council's website and searching 'adult education' or 'adult learning' in the search bar. You can also find courses in your area by searching on FindCourses findcourses.co .uk/search/fun-hobby-and-exercise-classes/

The WEA www.wea.org.uk/ have classes in almost every area of England and Scotland. On their website, they explain that you don't need any previous knowledge or qualifications to join most of their courses, only a willingness to share with others your curiosity, ideas, and experience.

If you are an older person and work part time or have retired, U3A u3a.org.uk/ has over 1000 locally run interest groups in the UK that provide a wide range of opportunities to come together and learn and explore new ideas, skills, and activities together. On their website, they state that U3A is 'local, social, friendly, low-cost and open to all. There's so much out there to experience – what's stopping you?'

Feeling the Fear and Doing It Anyway

In an interview with the *Guardian* newspaper in April 2018, Jacqueline Thomas, 52, described how, three years earlier, she'd moved to a village with her partner David. They didn't know anyone in the area so had to start getting to know other people from scratch. The variety of classes and groups that Jacqueline signed up for at the village hall was the start of some new friendships.

As well joining as the Women's Institute – which she says was one of the best decisions she made – Jacqueline, who is a wheelchair user, signed up for something that was completely new for her: an adapted martial arts class. She was surprised to find how much she enjoyed it. Encouraged by her teacher, Carl Hodgetts, who in 2006 became the first wheelchair-using kickboxing instructor in the UK, she now holds a white belt in Shiying Do adapted martial art. Jacqueline says that joining in with something that's new to you just takes one leap of faith. 'Even if you're absolutely terrified, do it,' she says, adding: 'Even I'm a bit shocked about the martial arts, though.' When it comes to making friends, Jacqueline's advice is 'Don't be afraid of being scared. Do it anyway.'

Like Jacqueline, Jessica Pan also tried something new. In an interview with BBC Radio 4's Woman's Hour, Jessica described how, in her year of trying out new activities and experiences, she took classes that scared her. 'When I did the comedy course I met amazing friends and on the improv course I met creative people that I would never have met otherwise.'

Jessica suggests that we're not always good at recognizing what we might actually like. 'I signed up for an eight-week improv course and I thought I'm going to hate this! (But) being on with these other strangers ... I absolutely loved it, it was so fun.'

If you're anxious about taking the first step – attending a new group and/or a new activity for the first time – ask a friend, family member, or colleague to come with you to an event or meet-up. Having a familiar face can help you to feel more confident. Just don't stay with them the whole time otherwise you'll never talk to anyone else!

Top Tip

Try it with no reason other than to see what it's like; like a scientist setting up an experiment for the purpose of discovering something unknown, join in with no expectations other than to see what happens as a result.

If it doesn't work out, try another one.

Groups Where the Specific Aim Is to Connect People

As well as the Meetup groups, courses, and classes in your area, there are national organizations with local groups. Below are a variety of groups and clubs whose specific aim is to bring people together so that they can connect and make friends.

Men's Sheds menssheds.org.uk/ are community spaces for men to connect, converse, and create. There are more than 300 Men's Sheds throughout the UK. They bring men together in a familiar and comfortable environment, working side by side fixing and making things. Members share the tools and resources they need to work on projects of their own choosing at their own pace. They are places of skill-sharing and informal learning, of individual pursuits and community projects, of purpose, achievement, and social interaction.

The Camden Town, London Men's Shed

Talking to Katy Hafner in 2016 for a *New York Times* article, Mike Jenn, a retired charity worker who runs a Men's Shed in London suggested that men have 'this kind of male pride thing. We say, "I can look after myself. I don't need to talk to anyone," and it's a complete fallacy. Not communicating helps to kill us.'

Keith Pearshouse, 70, a retired school head, discovered the Men's Shed near his home after moving to

London from Norfolk, and recognizing he was lonely. Amid the noise of a table saw, router, and lathe at the Camden Town shed – a 700-square-foot workshop in a local community centre – Keith told Katy that he had been a bit anxious about walking into a roomful of people for the first time, but he immediately realized, 'Yeah, this is a place that would work for me.' Keith had never worked with wood before he discovered the Men's Shed. The pieces he produces are gratifying, he told Katy, but not nearly as gratifying as the human connections he has made.

The Women's Institute thewi.org.uk/ is a community-based organization for women that offers a wide range of activities and interest-based events.

The Townswomen's Guild www.the-tg.com/, like The Women's Institute, offers friendship groups for women. Members meet to enjoy each other's company, develop friendships, to get involved with events and crafts, try new things, and to campaign on social issues.

Apps that Help People Connect with Others

Friender frienderapp.com/ is a swipe-type app, but the profiles you see aren't random. When you build your profile, you add your interests so that suggested matches have at least one interest or activity in common with you.

TogetherFriends www.togetherfriends.com/ is a friend-ship website just for women in the UK. The app helps you to make new friends by putting you in touch with like-minded women who share the same interests and live in the same area. Many of their members have recently moved to an area, retired, lost a partner, or divorced and are now looking to make new friends. By linking you to other women, you can find a friend to go to the theatre, go dog walking, or have a coffee with. If you need a travel companion, they can help with this too.

Peanut www.peanut-app.io/ is an app for mums to meet other mums; you can connect with mums, expectant mums and those trying to conceive to build friendships, ask questions, and find support.

Meet My Dog https://meetmydogapp.com/ is an app for dogs and their owners to meet each other's dogs and their owners. As the app says: 'Dogs want to play with their friends, just like us.'

Nextdoor nextdoor.co.uk/ connects neighbours to each other and to everything nearby. You can find out what people in your street or your local neighbourhood are doing, such as book clubs or local historical groups, local businesses, services, community updates, recommenda-tions, and stuff your neighbours are looking to sell or give away for free. It's a good way to get to know others and be part of your community.

The Chatty Café Scheme https://thechattycafescheme .com/uk/ encourages cafés and other venues such as pubs, libraries, and community centres to designate a Chatter & Natter table. This is where customers can sit if they are happy to talk to other customers. When you put in your location, Google will search for venues near you.

You might even consider becoming a Chatty Café ambassador at a Chatty Café venue. As an ambassador, you'll meet new people and help strengthen connections within your community. And, as they say on their website: 'Volunteer with us and get back a whole lot more than you give.'

Helplines and Support

The Silver Line www.thesilverline.org.uk/ is a free confidential helpline providing information, friendship, and advice to older people, open 24 hours a day, every day of the year, on 0800 470 80 90. Their free Telephone Friendship Service matches people aged 60 and over with a friendly volunteer for a weekly chat.

Side by Side https://sidebyside.mind.org.uk/ is a safe, moderated community where you can share your experiences of feeling lonely, anxious, depressed, and/or mental health problems.

Volunteer

Volunteering for a cause or local community initiative that interests you is another way to connect with other people and experience positive relationships. There are people you haven't even met yet who need you! Doing something to benefit someone else can make you and the person you are helping feel good. Studies show that helping others creates feelings and attitudes that can lead to better physical health, better mental health, and overall happiness.

Helping others creates a positive mindset. Why? Because you have to actively look for positive ways to reach out to help and support someone who is struggling or finding it difficult to cope. It gets you into a cycle of positive thinking and behaviour. You'll feel good for doing good in the world and see you are making a difference. It'll also give you something to talk about with new friends and family.

As well as helping and meeting others, you'll meet other volunteers who could become friends. You can meet and create bonds with people who want to make a contribution to the lives of others; you have a common cause that is an opportunity to connect with others.

Promote a Cause

You could get involved in a fundraising initiative; raising funds for cancer research, for example. A few years ago myself and three friends raised money for research into Parkinson's disease by joining a week-long sponsored walk (organized by

Parkinsons UK) along the Great Wall of China (only a section of it – not all 13,000 miles!) The individuals in the group were from all parts of the UK and, in the years since, several of us have kept in touch and met together for an annual walking holiday in England.

Volunteers can do almost anything; there's a huge range of volunteer opportunities available to you. Whether it's serving tea at a local hospice, helping at a local community food project or an animal rescue centre, working with refugees, advocating for someone with a learning disability or mental health problem, or mentoring people leaving the criminal justice system, not only can you do something of worth and value, but you can be involved in something that's relevant to your values and interests.

Try to find an activity that offers:

- A role relevant to your interests. It may be related to the environment, conservation, arts and music; or perhaps family and children, politics or the environment; or maybe some voluntary work with older people.
- An opportunity to use the skills you already have or one that provides training to learn new skills.
- The opportunity for regular helping: a couple of hours a week. Frequency of helping is important, because it's a regular opportunity to take the focus off yourself and your concerns.

If you're anxious about the first step to volunteering, you could ask a colleague, friend, or family member to join you as a fellow helper.

Fill the Times When You Feel Most Lonely

If there are times of the day, week, or year when feelings of loneliness are more intense, you might want to consider filling that time with some voluntary work.

After Harvey's partner died, Harvey found Sundays particularly difficult to get through; he felt his partner's absence particularly intensely on Sundays. So, he volunteered to work on Sunday afternoons at his local hospital. Not only did meeting and chatting to patients alleviate Harvey's loneliness but Harvey worked with other volunteers and made some new friends.

Greta had no family to spend Christmas with and although her friends often told her she was very welcome to join them, Greta chose instead to volunteer at her local animal shelter.

Volunteer outdoors The Conservation Volunteers tvc .org.uk/ and **The Wildlife Trusts** www.wildlifetrusts .org run outdoor volunteering projects around the UK. **The Social Farms & Gardens** website www.farmgarden .org.uk has details of community gardens and farms around the UK. And if you have a disability and want to start or continue gardening, **Thrive** www.thrive.org .uk can help.

Run! If you like running and are interested in volunteering, **The Good Gym** www.goodgym.co.uk/ is worth checking out. The Good Gym run groups that combine getting fit with doing good. You stop off on runs to do physical tasks for community organizations and to support isolated older people with social visits and one-off tasks they can't do on their own. It's a great way to motivate you to get fit, meet new people, and do some good by helping make your local area a better place to live.

The Real Junk Food Project www.realjunkfoodbrighton .co.uk/volunteer/ is an organization that uses food that would otherwise have been discarded from supermarkets and restaurants, to produce meals that are sold on a 'pay what you want' basis at pop-up junk food project community cafés around the UK.

The project also aims to help tackle social isolation and give people a sense of acceptance and belonging – one volunteer describes the joy she gets from speaking to people from all walks of life and, she says, 'feeling accepted for who I am'. Another volunteer says that 'as an introvert, I wouldn't speak to anyone for days, but I am able to interact here with no pressure'.

Having a disability doesn't need to be a barrier to volunteering. **Citizens Advice and Witness Service** www .citizensadvice.org.uk/, for example, has plenty of opportunities to volunteer. They welcome volunteers with a disability and volunteers with physical and mental health conditions.

Whatever your abilities, interests, and the amount of time you have available, the **Do It** website www.do-it .org/ allows you to search for all kinds of volunteering opportunities in the UK by entering your postcode or town.

You can also find out about volunteering opportunities near you by visiting your local volunteer centre or visiting www.volunteering.org.uk/ and www.ncvo.org.uk/

Develop the courage to think of others and to do something for them.

Dalai Lama

When you're lonely, it's easy to feel overwhelmed with your own concerns. But if you look beyond yourself and notice other people who need support or help, you may find that your loneliness takes a back seat. Help other people and, in the process, you help yourself; you bring a fresh perspective to your own life and circumstances.

> ### Helping Others to Help Yourself.
> ### The Marmalade Trust
>
> Amy Perrin is an occupational therapist and founder, in 2013, of the Marmalade Trust www.marmalade trust.org/ – a charity dedicated to raising awareness of loneliness and helping people make new friendships.

Amy is well aware of how tough social isolation and loneliness can be. At the age of 30, she moved to Bristol with her partner, but the relationship broke down. Amy found herself alone in a city 200 miles from her friends and family. Despite having a job to go to each day, weekends were empty. Amy realized she was lonely, but couldn't tell anyone. She felt embarrassed; that it wasn't something she could talk about.

It was volunteering that changed Amy's situation, when she started a monthly tea party for the charity Contact the Elderly. http://reengage.org.uk/ In an interview with the *Guardian* newspaper, in 2018, Amy explained: 'Through volunteering and meeting other volunteers, I built my confidence and when I got to work on Monday I had something to talk about. I was able to connect with my colleagues. And shifting my focus towards other people, not being so introspective, meant my mood improved. I felt I had a purpose and a mission to help other people feel less lonely.'

Walking Workout with a Difference

In 2017, after moving from London to Rochester in Kent, Sandra Samuels-Allen found herself feeling isolated and lonely; she had had no friends in the Medway area to hang out with and share life experiences with.

Thinking about how she was going to meet people she realized there might be others in her new community who were feeling isolated and lonely. 'I never talked about my loneliness to my family and friends,' says Sandra. 'I wanted to put into action something that would help others.'

So, she posted a message on Facebook, inviting others to join her for a walk and to talk. Much to her surprise, she had an overwhelming response; 50 people replied!

What started as a way of making friends has now grown into a much bigger event: 'Walking Workout with a Difference' www.walkingworkoutwithadiff erence.com/.

Offering a wide range of activities to support people of all ages and varying abilities, Walking Workout with a Difference has embraced the whole community and helped people develop new friendships.

Members meet twice a week to meet others, talk, walk, and enjoy being outdoors and in nature. Sandra is also a personal trainer and she organizes easy-going exercises during the group walking sessions.

'Some of the members are in relationships but still feel isolated and lonely. Some of their partners have disabilities, so it limits how often they can go out. Some members have anxiety, others have depression, but when they come to the group, all of that goes. 'We give each other support, including myself. Creating this group has been an amazing journey for all of us. We all connect with each other in different ways.'

> If you're interested in joining a local walking group, find one at Meetup www.meetup.com/ or go to www .ramblers.org.uk/

Remember, when you're involved doing something that you like and that has purpose and meaning for you, the opportunities to converse and to form connections will come more naturally.

Step Out of Your Comfort Zone

You might believe that it won't be easy, it'll take too long to meet people and make friends with them. It could be that you think 'I might not do it right.' It's true – it might be too hard, it will take some time and effort. But if you stay where you are, if you don't push yourself, nothing will change and you won't be happier.

Don't, for example, be like Ali. Ali figured that if he didn't try, if he didn't take any risks, then he couldn't fail. Although he really wanted to make some friends, Ali wasn't prepared to meet new people and to accept invitations to things he wouldn't normally have gone to. He felt that it might not be worth the time and effort. He certainly wasn't going to initiate a conversation. What if the other person was boring or stupid? Or what if he liked the other person but they weren't interested in him?

This was Ali's approach to most things in life – he took no risks. But by risking nothing – by staying in his comfort zone – Ali is trapped in his limited life. And he's not happy.

You can't change situations you don't take responsibility for. Sigmund Freud once said: 'Most people do not really want freedom, because freedom involves responsibility, and most people are frightened of responsibility.' It's the same with friendship; making and having friends involves responsibility. And time and effort.

If you're like Ali, the more you avoid making changes, the less likely it is that you'll move out of loneliness. You don't give yourself the chance to discover who and what might be out there, you don't learn how to manage challenges, and you don't give yourself the opportunity to feel good about yourself for having reached out to others. So you don't get to be happier.

It doesn't have to be this way!

Meeting new people and making friends does involve making an effort, persevering, taking some risks. It means stepping out of your comfort zone. But each time you extend your comfort zone you extend the possibility of connecting with other people and making friends.

Have Courage!

Courage is not the absence of fear but rather the determination that something else is more important.

Focus on the positive. Remind yourself what it is that you want; to connect with and get to know other people – people that you like and who like you. This can give you the motivation and courage you need to take the necessary first step. Focusing on why you're doing something and what you want to achieve, keeping that in your mind, can help stop feelings of doubt, uncertainty, and fear from taking over.

Rather than fight feelings of fear and doubt, acknowledge and accept them. Tell yourself 'I'm feeling scared. I'm not sure about this.' Then push past those thoughts and feelings and tell yourself 'But I can do this.' Feel the fear. And then do it.

Don't overthink it. The more you think about whether you should or shouldn't do something, the longer you have to come up with excuses, the less likely you are to take that first courageous step. Courage can be prone to leaking so the longer you wait, the less of it you'll have. Once you've decided to do something, don't wait, do it!

Focus on the first step. This might be going, for example, to that first Meetup meeting or making that call about voluntary work. So often, taking the first step is half the battle, so pushing yourself over the threshold will create the momentum that will move things forward. And by then you'll just be dealing with it.

Whether you take action or not, life will continue. So you might as well screw up your courage, take action, and make things work out so that, as life continues, it does so in the ways you want it to.

In a nutshell

- There are people who are open to meeting others and making friends too. You've just got to find them. It takes effort on your part; you need to be willing to meet others, to be yourself and give something of yourself.
- Getting together with people who enjoy the same things as you makes it easier for you to talk to them and make friends because you've already got something in common: shared values, a shared interest, and/or a shared identity.
- People who go to 'Meetups' do so knowing they'll be meeting people who are also open to meeting other people and making new friends. And, with any group, there are usually new members joining, so as well as the regulars, there's the potential to meet more people over the coming months.
- Do consider trying a new activity or sign up for a course to learn something new and meet new people.
- As well as the Meetup groups, courses, and classes in your area, find out about the national organizations with local groups whose specific aim is to bring people together so that they can connect and make friends.

- Volunteering for a cause or local community initiative that interests you is another way to connect with other people and experience positive relationships.
- If you're anxious about attending something for the first time, ask a friend, family member, or colleague to come with you. Just don't stay with them the whole time otherwise you'll never talk to anyone else!
- Focus on the positive; remind yourself what it is that you want: to connect with and get to know other people – people that you like and who like you. This can give you the motivation and courage you need to take the necessary first step.
- If any one event or group doesn't feel right, try another one.

5
Making Friends:
What to Do

Remember that every good friend was once a stranger.

Author unknown

Connecting with other people, then, requires that you actively set out to meet other people. But once you *have* started meeting new people, how do you turn those connections into friendships? The same way as you made the connections in the first place – with time and effort.

Jessica Pan, author of *Sorry I'm Late I Didn't Want to Come*, was scared of rejection. 'I thought,' she said, 'people don't want to talk to me; they won't like me or they will think I'm weird.' However, what changed things for Jessica was something a psychologist told her. He said: 'Nobody waves but everybody waves back.' 'So,' says Jessica, 'we really need to be that first person to do that move, make that wave. Ask someone for coffee and they almost always respond back in a good way.'

Of course, you can't make instant friendship happen but you can be willing to be the one to suggest a meet-up or get together.

Asking people to do something together outside of how and where you already know them or see each other helps to move a potential friendship forward. You might, for example, get on well with someone you work with. If you're interested in becoming better friends you could invite them to something outside of work. Or, in another example, if there are one or more people you like at a club you've been going to, you could suggest you do something together before or after a meeting. The same is true of anyone you know and get on with in a partic- ular context – a neighbour, for example, a parent whose child goes to the same school as yours, or someone who belongs to the same club or gym as you.

Just by getting to know the other person you will have learnt a bit about what their interests, likes, and dislikes are. You'll have an idea about what they'd like to do or might like to try out. So suggest you do it together. It could be going to a particular film, play, or comedy or music event. It might be to go and watch a sporting match together or to try out a sport or other activity. It could be a meal or a drink at the pub. It could be a day trip somewhere – to visit a garden or National Trust property. It could be to play a board game or video game together, or just simply watch a favourite show together. At the end of last year, I suggested my mum – aged 92 and living on her own – did a simple, easy thing: invite her neighbour, Pauline, to watch the final of

Strictly Come Dancing. They had a very enjoyable evening together. You can do the same (not necessarily invite your neighbour in to watch Strictly!) but take the initiative and suggest something simple and enjoyable to do together.

Eat with Someone Else

If you live on your own, you don't have to eat alone each and every day. Invite someone to eat with you – even if it's just a takeaway or a supermarket curry.

For a number of years, after they were both widowed and before director and actor Carl Reiner died in 2020, each evening, the director and actor Mel Brooks would drive from his home in Santa Monica to Carl's house in Beverly Hills. There, they did what they liked to do most: chat, eat dinner together and watch the long-running TV quiz show *Jeopardy!*

Think of Creative Ways to Spend Time with Others

As I write this book in the winter of 2020/21, the Covid pandemic has shown how so many people have come up with creative ways to meet up with others while staying safe. This has often meant relying on the outdoors for get-togethers. My friend Karen and I, for example, got together in a park in the town where she lives, and sat on a park bench with a takeaway pizza and prosecco one lunchtime.

Other friends of mine had games evenings with neighbours on either side of their ground-floor window. One family were outside in the garden, the other family inside their living room. They played charades and then Pictionary, using large pieces of paper and markers.

Pandemic or no pandemic, if you can't get together physically with other people, it's important to find ways to maintain connections.

There's a wide range of games, for example, that you can play with others, using Zoom. 'Heads Up!', 'GeoGuessr', and 'Psych' are just a few of the apps you can download and then play with others.

You could have a joint movie viewing where you watch on one screen while video chatting on another. The app Netflix Party www.netflixparty.com/ (now renamed Teleparty) is a way to do this. The app synchronizes video playback and adds group chat to Netflix, Disney, Hulu, and HBO. You might choose something neither of you has watched or schedule a weekly date watching one another's favourite films, together or separately, and talk about them afterwards.

Someone I know kept in touch with her son by making the same recipe together via Zoom once a week, chatting as they made the recipe and then comparing the finished dish.

Whether you're getting together with others virtually or online, think of the things you like to do or new things you'd like to try and ask someone to join you.

Of course, you don't have to invite just one person. If you know two, three, or more people from a particular place – work, a club or Meetup group you go to – rather than invite one person to do something with you, you might find it easier to invite a couple of people out or over to your house for curry or pizza, or each person bring a dish. Or you could suggest a few of you do a city or country walk and a pub lunch or all go to an event related to your shared interests.

Top Tip

Meet your friends' friends. One of the easiest ways to make new friends and expand your social circle is to meet your friends' friends. So ask a friend to invite one or two of their friends to join you the next time you do something together.

Let Friendships Develop Naturally

Don't expect too much. A common mistake is expecting too much from one person. It's less intense for you and others if you make friends with a number of different people – individuals with different interests and backgrounds. Aim to make different friends for different reasons.

Taking It Slowly

Sunita has a strong, happy relationship with her partner. She has two good friends she's known for years and who live in her home town 50 miles from where Sunita now lives. However, Sunita struggles to make new friends – she's found that each time she's changed job or moved, although she looks forward to getting to know other people and becoming friends, something – she's never sure what – seems to go wrong.

On a visit back to her home town, she met up with her friend Phil and talked to him about it. 'I do meet nice people – people I hope I could be friends with – interesting and fun people and we get on for a while, but slowly and surely I feel myself being pushed away. Texts go unanswered and invitations are turned down. The friendship fizzles out before it's really got going.'

Sunita told Phil that since her eldest child started at his new school, she'd begun to get to know some of the parents at her son's school, whom she liked. 'I've taken steps towards making friends, but I'm worried that I'll mess it up again.'

Phil had some good advice; he suggested Sunita try not to go into situations regarding every new person as a potential friend. 'The fact that you have children at the same school as other parents is a good start, but maybe you're expecting too much of new friends, too soon? Friendships need time to develop. If you come across as too eager to be friends you can actually push people away.'

It's true; if others feel that you're looking for too much from them too soon, they'll back away. The process of moving from saying hello, having brief chats, to doing things together, then doing interesting, fun things together, sharing more of your lives and details of your lives can take time.

As Phil went on to explain: 'Either friendships develop naturally or they don't. It's good to initiate them, you've only messed up if you try and move a friendship along too quickly; you could come across as pushy or needy. Play dates with your son and his friends and asking their parent in for a coffee when they collect them are a good start, but don't try and rush it. Getting to know someone slowly also means that if you do realise that actually, they're not your kind of person, then you're not the one in the awkward position of having to back away.'

Making new friends means putting yourself out there, and that can be scary. It's especially intimidating if you're someone who, in the past, has been let down or badly treated by others.

It's not always easy to know if someone is open to spending time with you and developing a friendship. Although you don't want to come across as pushy or needy, to get to know someone better and make friends you have to reach out – just be prepared to risk rejection. But, by gathering up a bit of courage and taking those first few steps, new people and acquaintances *can* become friends.

And if someone does turn you down? Or they do accept your invite to do something with you but afterwards, they don't seem interested in doing something together again? It doesn't mean they're rejecting you as a person. They may have other things going on in their lives; a lot of other commitments so that they may not have the time and/or the emotional space for new friends right now. Give yourself credit for trying and think what, if anything, you learned from the experience.

And, finally, be the friend that you would like to have. Treat potential friends just as you want them to treat you: be honest, reliable, thoughtful, trustworthy.

In a nutshell

- Turning new connections into friendships takes time and effort.
- As the saying goes, 'The road and the phone run both ways.' So don't just wait for others to invite you to do things, be willing to be the one to suggest doing something together.
- Having spent time talking and getting to know someone, you'll have learnt a bit about what their interests, likes, and dislikes are. You'll have an idea about what they'd like to do or might like to try out.

- You could do something before or after work, the school run, a meeting, event, or activity you've both attended. Simply take the initiative and suggest something simple and enjoyable to do together.
- You don't have to invite just one person. If you know two or three people from a particular place – work, a club or Meetup group you go to – organize something you could all do together.
- Aim to make friends with a number of different people – individuals with different interests and backgrounds.
- If you can't get together physically with other people, think outside the box; find other ways to maintain connections.
- Although you don't want to come across as pushy or needy, to get to know someone better and make friends you have to reach out – just be prepared to risk rejection.
- But, by gathering a bit of courage and taking those first few steps, new people and acquaintances can become friends.
- If someone does turn you down, it doesn't mean they're rejecting you as a person. They may have other things going on in their lives.
- Give yourself credit for trying and think what, if anything, you learned from the experience.

6
Making Friends: What to Say

Be who you are and say what you feel, because those who mind don't matter and those who ·matter don't mind.

Dr Seuss

Whether it's just a minute waiting for an elevator with a colleague, or waiting in the playground with another parent for your children to come out of school or a few hours sat next to a friend's cousin at a wedding, with some people you feel comfortable talking to them and conversation just seems to flow quite naturally. But with others, it's not so easy; trying to engage the other person is like pushing a piano uphill; it's hard work. What to say? What to ask? How to respond? What if there's an awkward silence?

For many of us, chatting to others doesn't come easily, particularly if your experience of loneliness has left you low on confidence and self-esteem. Perhaps you worry that you'll come across as weird or dull and the other person won't want to engage with you. But maybe you're not concerned with how you come across, it's more that you think small talk is shallow or boring; that it feels fake and a waste of time and that there's more to life than talking about the weather or the price of fish. Maybe so. But small talk can (although it doesn't have to) lead to big things! Sure, it might start with the obvious comments and pleasant exchanges but small talk serves an important purpose – it establishes the foundation for conversations in which interesting views, experiences, and ideas can be exchanged.

Small talk is simply about connecting; to come across as an approachable, friendly person who is open to exchanging a few pleasantries. You don't have to impress, you don't have to be brilliant. You just have to be nice. Smile, ask questions, listen, take a genuine interest in the other person and say something about yourself. Here are some guidelines to help you feel more confident:

Make the first move. Initiating conversation is a bold step, but you just need to smile and say, 'Hi, I'm ... What's your name?'

Be positive. Don't start off with a moan or a complaint; say something positive.

Don't worry about coming up with clever conversation starters or having the 'right' thing to say. It doesn't matter if you make the usual comments 'It's so cold today!' or questions; 'How do you know Maria?' or 'Have you been here before?' or 'What do you do/where do you work?' but you do need to be interested in and follow up on their answers. So show an interest in the other person, their world, and what they might be interested in. Ask them about something that you notice about them. 'I see you came by bike. Do you do a lot of cycling?'

Comment or ask their opinion on something that both you and the other person are experiencing; where you're both at and what's around you. For example, say 'I really love this restaurant.' It's likely they'll ask you why, which opens up another opportunity for conversation. And if they don't, ask what they think of the place.

Be bold. Just about anything you find curious or interesting can start a conversation and keep things rolling. Maybe you read or heard about something interesting, something useful in the last few days. Maybe you heard an intriguing theory? Tell them then ask their opinion about it.

You can draw on stories from anywhere, from stories that happened to people you know, to those you came across in the news, on the radio, a podcast, TV, magazines and so on. If they stuck in your mind, they must have been engaging to you. So they're good to share as just that: something that struck you as interesting, strange, or funny. Tell it and then ask their opinion.

Ask for advice. As the 19th-century writer Arthur Helps observed: 'We all admire the wisdom of those who come to us for advice.' Using conversation openers that acknowledge the other person's skills, knowledge, or experience such as 'You've worked for that company – would you recommend them as a good company to work for?' or 'You go to Glastonbury each year – where's the best area to camp?' is a good way to connect and get a conversation going. You learn something new and the other person gets to feel included and their expertise is acknowledged. (But don't ask someone for their professional advice at a social event. For example, at your cousin's wedding, don't ask another guest who's a doctor what they think about the rash on your leg!)

Top Tip

Imagine They're Already a Friend

Still feeling apprehensive? Imagine that the other person is already your friend. You know a friend would respond positively if you approached them so pretend this person is already a friend.

Don't worry if you forget a name. It will help you to remember a person's name later in the conversation if you repeat their name when you are introduced to them: 'Nice to meet you, Madonna'. If you later find that you've forgotten her name, admit it. 'Gosh, I'm sorry, can you remind me of your name?' Once they've told you, don't make a big deal of it, simply repeat their name and move on with the conversation. 'Madonna. Thanks. Well, as I was saying . . . ' It won't be nearly as tough as you think!

Ask questions. After the first few exchanges between you, you can keep the conversation flowing by asking more questions. Ask open questions that require more than a 'yes' or 'no' answer and give the other person an opportunity to talk about themselves, their opinions or experiences. Good questions involve asking someone what they think or how they feel about whatever it is they're talking about. Even simple things like 'What was that like?' or 'How did it feel?' can keep people talking.

Top Tip

When someone tells you about something they've been doing or have experienced, ask them, 'What was the best thing about it?' and 'What was the worst thing about it?' 'Why?'

If you've listened well, you can use any unexplored topics touched on earlier in the conversation to keep things moving. For instance, you might say, 'Earlier, you mentioned ... can you tell me more about that?'

And if you've met and talked to someone before, try to remember something about them that you can ask them about; ask them about something they mentioned before. They might, for example, have told you about what was currently happening in their life or something they were planning on doing. Ask them how things turned out. 'Last time we met you were training to be a driving instructor. How's that been going?'

Here are some more ideas for questions you can ask to start a conversation or keep it going:

Work

- What was your first ever job?
- What was the best or worst job you've ever had? Why?
- What do you enjoy most and least about your current job?
- If you weren't working here, where would you like to be working? Why?
- Would you rather work four 10-hour days or five eight-hour days? Why?
- When you were a child, what did you think you were going to do when you grew up – was it this job?

Entertainment

- If you could only watch one genre of movies/books for the rest of your life, what would it be? Why?
- Who are your favourite film stars/solo artists/bands? What do you like about them?
- What's the last good book you read? What's the last good TV show or series you watched? What was good about it?
- Do you listen to podcasts? Are there any you'd recommend?
- Do you like going to the cinema or prefer watching at home? Why?
- What's your favourite board game? Why?

Food

- Which meal is your favourite: breakfast, lunch, or dinner? Why?
- If you could only eat three things for the rest of your life, what would they be? Why?
- What's the weirdest thing you've ever eaten?
- What are your favourite comfort foods? Why?

Travel

- If you could fly and stay anywhere for free, where would you go? Why?
- What's the best and worst holiday you've been on? Why?
- If you could take six months' paid leave, where would you go and what would you do? Why?
- Where's the last place you travelled to ? What did you do there?
- What's the next trip you have planned?

Random

- What would be your ideal superpower? Invisibility? To be able to fly? To breathe underwater? To see in the dark? To be able to mind-read? Omnilingualism (the ability to speak any language)? Atmokinesis (the ability to control the weather)?
- What talent or skill would you like to have – to sing, play a musical instrument, play a sport, draw or paint?
- If you could have any type of animal for a pet, what would it be? Why?

- Do you think everyone should know how to swim? Why?
- Ideally, how would you spend your birthday?
- What's your favourite season, and why?
- Have you ever disliked something and then changed your mind?
- Are there any apps on your phone that you can't live without? (A couple of years ago, at a party, someone asked me this question and I explained that twice a year I lead walking holidays in Europe and that I couldn't live without the map app that I use. The other person was interested and asked me all about it. Our conversation led him to contacting the organization I work for and going on to be a walk leader himself.)

The greatest compliment that was ever paid me was when one asked me what I thought, and attended to my answer.

Henry David Thoreau

Listen for something in the other person's reply that might suggest a direction for the conversation to take. Follow up on what the other person says. Ask 'How come?' 'Why's that?' 'Why not?' 'What was that like?' Ask questions and, more importantly, listen and respond to the answers.

Top Tip

Ask Questions

Don't be afraid to ask questions if you're unsure or not clear about something the other person is telling you. Asking questions does not make you look stupid. You just need to listen to news programmes and chat shows on the radio and TV to know this; note how often the interviewer asks questions to clarify both their own and the listener's or viewer's understanding.

The next step is to draw on your own experience or knowledge of what the other person is talking about without taking over the conversation and turning it into it being all about you! Communication is about an exchange of thoughts, ideas, opinions, etc. A conversation is like a jam session in jazz, where one starts with conventional elements and then spontaneous variations occur that take things in a new direction.

Say Something About Yourself; Your Ideas, Experiences, Opinions

Although you might be genuinely interested in what the other person has to say, if you keep firing out questions the other person will feel that they're being interrogated!

'How do you know Rob?' 'What do you do?' 'Where do you work?' 'Where are you from?' 'Where do you live now?' That's too many questions in one go.

If you're talking to someone new and you've been asking them about themselves, at some point, you must say something about yourself. Maybe, though, you hesitate to talk about yourself; you're not comfortable with opening up and you find it easier to let the other person talk about themselves. But communication is a two-way process – it involves an *exchange* of ideas, information, feelings, etc., so you'll need to make a contribution yourself. Be willing to share a bit of yourself; who you are, what you do, what you do and don't like and find interesting, etc.

Top Tip

Say Something

Did you lose your keys today or find £10? Tell the other person, then ask if they've ever done the same. You could say something about a book you're reading, or an app you've found useful. What about a film, TV show, or box set you've recently watched? Tell the other person and ask if they've read or watched something good recently. Maybe you ate at a new restaurant last week, or heard some great new music. Tell the other person then ask if they've had a similar experience. This is the key – to follow up something you've said about yourself with a question about their opinion or experience in a similar situation.

Often, awkward silences appear in conversation because you are worried about saying the 'right' thing and you hold back from saying something because you're not sure if it's clever or interesting enough. What does that do to the potential for conversation? It kills it!

Just say whatever comes to your mind. No asking yourself 'What would they think if I say this?' None of that. Say it. Then ask them what they think. Remember that this step is the crucial part – follow up what you've said with a relevant question, If you feel like talking about the pizza you had for breakfast, do that. If you follow it up with a question 'What's the weirdest thing you've had for breakfast?' then you've opened up the conversation. You'll discover that it's actually fine to let go and talk about whatever you feel like.

As my niece Olivia – one of the most likeable, friendly, fun people I know – says: 'You can always think of something – say what comes into your head and then see how the other person responds. Then take it from there.'

Top Tip

Talk Positively About Other People

Try a little 'spontaneous trait transference'. When you talk about another person, listeners unconsciously associate you with the characteristics you're describing. 'Say positive and pleasant things about

---

friends and colleagues, and you are seen as a nice person', advises Professor Richard Wiseman in his book *59 Seconds: Think a Little, Change a Lot.*

Keep the Conversation Going

When the other person asks you a question, respond with more than the minimum; give the other person something to pick up on. Here are some examples:

Question: 'How are you?' Short response: 'Fine.' Response that leads to further conversation: 'Good, thanks. I'm looking forward to next week – I'm going on holiday to Italy.'

Question: 'Where are you from?' Short response: 'Brighton.' Response that leads to further conversation: 'I'm from Brighton. Have you ever been to Brighton? You have? What did you like about it?'

Question: 'What did you do this weekend?' Short response: 'I went house-hunting.' Response that leads to further conversation: 'I went house-hunting. We're thinking about moving out to the country.'

Talking about yourself and sharing your thoughts and opinions doesn't mean, though, that you should monopolize conversations. Be careful not to pontificate or lecture others on a cause or issue you care about. Over-explaining – sharing too much information, being too open and boring people with unnecessary details – can quickly turn someone else's initial interest into agony as they're dying for you to stop and they tell themselves to avoid you next time!

Don't panic when there's a lull in the conversation. Don't feel the need to rush in and fill the void. Sometimes silence is appropriate. You don't want to seem like a babbling idiot! Often, the other person will start talking.

Otherwise, take the conversation in a new direction. Throw something out there; just choose any one of the questions or topics of conversation described in the last few pages and don't worry about making the transition smooth.

If you do sense that the other person wants to get away, give them the opportunity to do so. For example, at a social event, you might say ... 'I expect you want to talk to some others – I'm going to the loo – maybe chat again later.'

Finally, know when to stop and pull out. If the conversation feels like climbing a hill of sand then it may be time to move on or let silence take over. You can't connect with everyone, and some conversations simply refuse to take life! ... Either way, end the conversation with something nice. For example, 'It was nice talking to you' or 'Have a good evening.'

Build Your Confidence

If you want to feel more comfortable and confident about making small talk, you'll need to practise.

Get into the habit of talking to people everywhere you go; challenge yourself to talk to an average of one new person a day, every day, for the next couple of weeks. At a shop, café, bar or restaurant, cinema or theatre, with anyone who works with the public, because they're used to people making small talk.

You could say something to a cashier in a supermarket. Look for a cashier who you can see chatting to a customer and so is open to remarks. 'It's quite busy/not very busy here today. Why's that do you think?' Or a charity collector, put some money in the collection tin and ask 'I expect you've been on your feet a long time already – how long will you be here today?' Acknowledge a neighbour and stop to exchange a few words. On the phone talking to someone at a call centre, ask what part of the country or what country they're speaking from. Ask what the weather is like there. At work, make a point of talking to someone you don't usually chat to. Talk to people who work in a different department from you.

Don't wait to feel confident about talking with other people before you start talking. The only way you'll feel more comfortable and confident talking to people is to do it frequently. What's the worst that can happen? Yes, you may be rebuffed or rejected, but feel the fear and do it anyway. By the time you've got over the fear, making small talk will be a habit. A good habit!

> **Top Tip**
>
> Practise Chatting to Others
>
> If you need practise chatting to new people, try dialup.com/ Whether it's discussing what book you're reading, what you're making for breakfast, the full moon, or world affairs, Dialup will ring your phone and another Dialup member's phone on an automated schedule and pair you randomly in a one-on-one conversation.

Do confident people ever feel anxious about communicating with other people? Yes, they do, but the difference between them and people lacking in confidence is that rather than focus on how much fear or anxiety they feel, confident people make use of their courage; they communicate with other people despite their trepidation. They recognize they have to start somewhere.

Talk to new people often enough and you'll eventually get comfortable making small talk and starting a conversation. Yes, it will feel strange and scary at first. And sometimes people will blank you. That's OK. They've got stuff going on and you don't know what it is. It's not you!

But after you've done this 10 times, 20 times, 30 times, it'll feel normal and natural. And who knows where it'll lead?

In a nutshell

- Small talk is simply about connecting. You don't have to impress, you just have to be nice. Smile, ask questions, listen, take a genuine interest in the other person, and say something about yourself.
- Don't worry about having the 'right' thing to say. It doesn't matter if you make the usual comments or ask the usual questions, but you do need to be interested in and follow up on their response.
- Keep the conversation going; draw on your own experience or knowledge of what the other person is talking about. Say something about yourself; share your ideas, experiences, opinions.
- When the other person asks you a question, respond with more than the minimum; give the other person something to pick up on.
- Don't monopolize conversations. Be sensitive to the other person's reactions to what you're saying. Their facial expressions and body language will tell you how they're feeling about what you're saying.
- If the conversation feels like climbing a hill of sand then it may be time to move on or let silence take over.
- The only way you'll feel more comfortable and confident talking to people is to do it frequently. Yes, it will feel strange and scary at first. And sometimes people will blank you. That's OK. They've got stuff going on and you don't know what it is. It's not you.

7
Fitting In

Not fitting in just means you're in the wrong place.

Author unknown

Even though you might meet with other people, take part in social activities and events, and have people in your life that you consider as friends, you might feel like you don't really fit in; you're like a round peg in a square hole.

Perhaps, in a range of situations or with some people, you feel like you're an outsider. It could be that you feel different from others in some way, or a number of ways. You may think that people don't really 'get' you or who you really are.

Spending time with people you don't feel close to can leave you feeling lonely.

No doubt you've heard the cliché about feeling lonely in a crowd. It might be a cliché but so often – like all clichés – it's true. Another cliché is that hell can be other people. And in a slight twist, loneliness, as well as hell, can be other people.

Loneliness isn't [just] the physical absence of other people ... it's the sense that you're not sharing anything that matters with anyone else. If you have lots of people around you ... but you don't share anything that matters with them, then you'll still be lonely.

Johann Hari

Are You Trying Too Hard?

It's natural to want others to understand us – our feelings and experience. But fitting in and feeling that you belong doesn't only come from being accepted by others. It starts with accepting and being yourself. Your true self. Too often we can try to be someone we're not – you might, for example, try too hard to be funny or show that you know a lot, that you're clever – in order to be liked, accepted, and fit in.

Of course, to a certain extent in different contexts and with different people – older family members, for example, children, colleagues, people in authority, or someone who is vulnerable – we adjust our behaviour accordingly in order to fit in or accommodate the other person. On the other hand, it's easy to be overly concerned with what others think of you, with the result that you try to be someone you're not.

Party Animal. Not

Writing in the *Guardian* newspaper in March 2020, in an article titled 'Parties make me feel like an alien in a person suit – and drinking to survive them didn't help', Gareth McLean described the 'countless occasions' that he'd embarrassed and humiliated himself at parties which he had endured because he thought he *had* to enjoy parties and that he needed to show that he was sociable, fun, and gregarious.

However, after one too many humiliations, Gareth turned down the invitations to drinks parties, screenings, soirees, and shindigs; he gave up drinking and learned to accept himself.

Now, he goes to very few parties, and when he does, he has a different attitude and approach. Gareth described how, at a recent party 'probably for the first time, I really enjoyed myself. I did not think this was possible at a party. And yet there I was … But there was something different this year … What was different? What had changed? That would be me.'

Gareth explained that the main difference was that he wasn't trying to have fun. He wasn't looking for approval and validation from others. Instead, he spent the evening simply chatting with people.

Gareth says now: 'I can look back at previous parties and make light of them, package them as anecdotes, so they can sound almost harmless, my trials trivial. But at the time, they were awful. Feeling like an

alien in a person suit is not a nice way to be. It's
lonely, relentless and exhausting ... I hold on to
the new me, who only goes to parties for the right
reason.'

Like Gareth, you may think that to be accepted and liked
you have to be someone you're not. But doing that will
leave you with unsatisfactory relationships and a sense
that no one really accepts or understands you.

Rather than act like you're someone else, you need to do
quite the opposite. You need to act yourself. As Dr Seuss
said: 'Today you are you, that is truer than true. There
is no one alive who is you'er than you.'

But how do you know who and what your true self is?
By identifying what your values are.

No doubt you'll have heard the exhortation to 'be true
to yourself!' and you may have wondered what exactly
that means; how do you be true to yourself? By living
your life according to your values. Then you are being
true to yourself.

Maybe you've not given much thought to what your
values are, but that doesn't mean you don't have them.
Quite simply, your values are what's important to you
and has some worth to you in the way that you live,
work, and relate to other people.

Know What's Important to You; Identify Your Values

What do you value? To help you identify your values, here is a list of some common core values. Tick any that are important to you. Add any you think of that are not included on the list:

Accountability
Achievement
Adventure
Affection
Altruism
Ambition
Amusement
Appreciation
Approval
Balance
Beauty
Belonging
Calmness
Care
Certainty
Clarity
Commitment
Compassion
Confidence
Contributing
Control
Cooperation
Courage

Courtesy
Creativity
Curiosity
Decisiveness
Dependability
Determination
Dignity
Directness
Discipline
Discretion
Duty
Empathy
Enjoyment
Equality
Excellence
Fairness
Family
Fidelity
Freedom of speech
Fun
Independence
Integrity

Justice
Kindness
Loyalty
Open-mindedness
Optimism
Peace
Perfection
Persistence
Privacy
Professionalism
Punctuality
Reliability
Respect
Security
Self-reliance
Simplicity
Sincerity
Spirituality
Spontaneity
Stability
Structure
Success
Support
Trust
Truth
Understanding
Unity

Once you've been through the list, narrow it down to between five and seven values. These are your 'core' values: your most important, essential values.

Some of your values are likely to be personal values; values that are concerned with how you behave and respond to situations; values such as optimism, clarity, privacy, or security. You will probably also have social values – values such as compassion, fairness and cooperation, reliability or honesty – which concern the way you interact with other people. You may have more personal values than social values. You may have more social values than personal values. It doesn't matter – whatever your values, they are what are important to *you*.

What have your values got to do with fitting in and feeling that you belong? When you're with people who either have similar values to you, or respect that your values are different to theirs, then in your interactions with them, you're able to be your true self; you can be real, genuine, and authentic. You feel that there is a mutual respect and understanding. You feel that you fit in.

On the other hand, when you are with people whose values are different from yours and there is little or no respect for each other's different values, it's a struggle to fit in and feel comfortable with that person or people because what matters to you isn't so important to them. And vice versa.

An example of different values could be where two people have different political or religious beliefs. Another example concerns work values – what's important to you about what you put into and get out of your job, your work or career may be very different to someone else's work values. And in another example, family values can differ; what you feel is important about how family members interact – values concerning duty and loyalty, truth and honesty, caring and compassion, etc. – may be different from another person's family values.

So, if there are certain people you feel less comfortable with than others, knowing that having similar values to someone else is what helps you to like each other and get on can help you understand why some people just aren't your type; why you don't feel that you fit in with them. There's nothing wrong with either of you – you just have different values, beliefs, and expectations from each other.

There's always going to be someone and some groups of people you won't fit in with. But that's not a problem if you're able to be who you truly are. Then, fitting in might not be so important. Why? Because the more you are able to accept yourself, to be who you are and do the things you like – things you want to do, that interest you and matter to you – the more likely others like you, who feel the same way and have the same interests and values, will be drawn to you. There *are* other square pegs out there!

Self-Acceptance

In a 2014 article for *The Huffington Post*, Liberty Forrest described how, as far back as she could remember, she found it difficult to fit in. Liberty wrote that no matter how hard she tried, nothing quite worked. 'I didn't think like other people. And I was often misunderstood. Sometimes I could learn to say and do enough of what was expected of me that I could pass for belonging on the outside. But I never felt it on the inside. The closest I ever got to "fitting in" was in my private moments of meditation, yoga, or other pursuits that connected me spiritually.'

Liberty learned that there's nothing wrong with her; that she's not flawed or defective. 'Just because other people do not understand me. I am simply a square peg in a round hole, full stop. The only acceptance I need is my own.'

There will still be some people in your life – even those you hold dear – who aren't always going to 'get' you. And that's OK. Rather than try and fit in with people and activities that are not really you, like Liberty Forrest, you may need to recognize that the only acceptance you need is your own.

In a nutshell

- It's natural to want others to understand us – our feelings and experiences – but fitting in and feeling that you belong doesn't only come from being accepted by others. It starts with accepting and being yourself.
- It's easy to be too concerned with what others think of you, with the result that you try to be someone you're not. Rather than act like you're someone else, you need to do quite the opposite. You need to act yourself.
- Being true to yourself is all about identifying and living your life according to your values. Your values are what's important to you and has some worth to you in the way that you live, work, and relate to other people.

- When you are with people whose values are different from yours it can be a struggle to fit in and feel comfortable with other people because what matters to you isn't so important to them. And vice versa.
- There's nothing wrong with you or them; you just have different values, beliefs, and expectations from each other.
- When you're with people who either have similar values to you, or respect that your values are different to theirs, you're able to be your true self; you can be real, genuine, and authentic. You fit in.
- The more you are able to accept yourself – to be who you are and do the things you like, things you want to do, that interest you and matter to you – the more likely others like you, who feel the same way and have the same interests and values, will be drawn to you.
- There will still be some people in your life – even those you hold dear – who aren't always going to 'get' you. And that's OK.

8
Getting Closer

Some people go to priests, others to poetry, I to my friends.

Virginia Woolf

When it comes to friendships and relationships, quality can be just as important as quantity. Feeling connected isn't just about how many or how few people you know or how little or how often you meet up. You can feel lonely because the relationship or relationships aren't as good – as deep, meaningful, or significant – as you would like them to be. You don't feel close – you don't feel that you have a shared understanding and empathy.

So how do you develop close friendships? By being prepared to open up and be more open to others.

You don't have to jump in and reveal your deepest hopes, thoughts, and fears but you do need to share something that's a bit more personal than you might normally share. And then see how the other person responds.

Be honest and sincere; talk about what you think and how you feel about things. Tell someone if you've been feeling, for example, sad and upset, jealous, envious, anxious, or regretful. If you're struggling with something that's going on in your life, tell the other person about it and maybe ask for advice. Simply ask: 'What do you think?' or 'Has that ever happened to you or anyone you know?' or 'What would you do?' If the other person readily offers their thoughts, ideas, and understanding you can feel encouraged that you've started to make a closer connection.

Be sure, though, not to use confiding in others – over-disclosing too early – revealing vulnerabilities, flaws, and secrets – as a strategy to endear yourself to someone. It could come off as needy.

Top Tip

Ask for Help When You Need It

Although it may seem uncomfortable at first to reach out, asking for and accepting help and support often makes friendships closer. If someone does offer advice and help, make sure you express your appreciation; the other person knowing that their efforts have been acknowledged and appreciated is a step towards a closer relationship.

As well as asking for and accepting help, do offer support as well to colleagues and neighbours. When times get tough, reach out. Don't wait for them to ask for help.

As well as what you may be struggling with, tell the other person your goals and what's going well; what you're pleased or happy about in your life right now. Tell them something you've learnt about yourself, about others, or your interactions with other people.

Do they seem interested? Do they ask questions about you, as if they'd like to get to know you better?

Do they tell you things about themselves?

If they don't tell you much about themselves, ask. Ask people about themselves. Find out more about what they've achieved and what challenges they've overcome. Ask how they feel about something they tell you about. Be interested. Be genuinely interested; don't waste their time and yours if you're not really interested and don't really care about that person, their thoughts, feelings, and opinions.

If the other person doesn't seem interested in what you have to say or they're not forthcoming with talking about themselves, that's OK. Everyone has their limits; maybe, for whatever reason, they won't or can't provide the interest and closeness that you're seeking.

On the other hand, you need to be careful not to misunderstand or misinterpret the attention of others.

Dating Scams

In loneliness there can be such a longing to fill the empty time and space and to find warmth and closeness that you can easily be drawn to anyone who shows interest. You may make yourself vulnerable to those whose motives are not genuine and sincere; people who aren't good for you.

Quite simply, if you are looking for love and a long-term relationship, you risk becoming a target for scammers. Meeting someone you think may be 'the one' can be exciting, but it can also lead to heartbreak and financial loss.

The term 'catfish' describes someone who creates fake personal profiles on social sites using someone else's pictures and false biographical information to pretend to be someone else. These catfishing scammers take advantage of people looking for romantic partners on dating websites, apps, or social media. They look to build relationships for the sole purpose of getting another person's money and/or their personally identifiable information.

Victim of a Dating Scam

Kelly had a good job in local government that she enjoyed. She had a small group of friends 'but,' she says, 'I was looking for that missing piece. I was emotionally lonely. I realise now that made me emotionally vulnerable.' Unfortunately, like thousands of others, Kelly fell victim to a cruel online romance scam, parting with thousands of pounds only to discover the man was a fraud.

In 2020, more than 6000 British lonely hearts – people of all ages – reported losses of £68 million to Action Fraud about fake foreign boyfriends. It's not just women that get conned, men are increasingly falling victim to the fraudsters too.

Kelly met 'Joe' online, on a dating app. 'He told me he was a US soldier stationed in Afghanistan and kept telling me I was beautiful and he was in love with me. His attention made me feel wanted and appreciated.' Her friends warned her that it was a scam but Kelly refused to listen, believing the man was genuine.

Joe love-bombed Kelly, sending her flowers and chocolates. He told her he couldn't wait to meet her. 'He said he wanted to come over for Christmas and spend the holidays with me but couldn't afford it. I sent him £2,000 believing it would be spent on booking flights. I took out a loan to cover it.

I was so excited. But when I went to meet him at the airport, he didn't turn up. Back home the next day, I did some research and I found out my gorgeous military man was actually a scammer in West Africa who had stolen a US soldier's photo and identity via Facebook, to draw me in.

Friends were sympathetic but one or two told me that it was my own fault that I'd been taken in and I was stupid for letting it happen. Not only did I lose money but my self-esteem and confidence took a big hit; the experience really knocked me back.'

The consequences of these scams are often financially and emotionally devastating to victims; they rarely get their money back and may not have the ability to recover from the financial loss. The UK governments's Money Advice Service www.moneyadviceservice.org .uk/ has advice on how to spot and avoid online dating scams.

It's not just romance scammers, though, that aren't good for you. A negative relationship with a friend, colleague, or family member can also be harmful and leave you feeling isolated and lonely. It might be someone you know who is unreliable, for example, or someone who criticizes you, or who takes advantage of your kindness and your generosity or is easily offended. It could be someone who brings unwanted drama or negative influences into your life.

The secret, darling, is to love everyone you meet. From the moment you meet them. Give everyone the benefit of the doubt. Start from a position that they are lovely and that you will love them. Most people will respond to that and be lovely and love you back and it becomes a self-fulfilling prophecy, and you can then achieve the most wonderful things. But get rid of any of the bastards that let you down.

Joanna Lumley

It's true what Joanna Lumley says – most people *are* lovely. But there are lots of people who are not. Other people can often be seen as either 'radiators' or 'drains':

radiators spread warmth and positivity, while drains take away your energy and resources; they can leave you feeling – amongst other things – discouraged, disappointed or angry, guilty or resentful. Their misery, criticism, and complaining can overwhelm you with negativity.

Surround yourself with goodness. I learned early on how to get the haters out of my life.

Michelle Obama

Who you spend most of your time with can make a big difference to the way you think, feel, and behave.

You need radiators – positive people – in your life! Positive people are likely to respond to you in positive ways and so make you think positively about yourself and the world around you.

Even if you can't remove 'the bastards that let you down' – the negative people from your life – what you *can* do is be aware of the effect their negativity is having on you and, as much as possible, reduce the amount of time you spend around them.

Steer clear of the moaners and the criticizers. Hanging out with negative-minded people who do nothing but complain will only drag you down and drain your energy. Avoid the negative people and increase the amount of time you spend with radiators, the positive people you know.

When looking to make new friends, you're looking for positive people! People who you can be yourself with, who make you feel good about yourself; who listen to you and encourage you.

Anyone who fits one or more of these descriptions is likely to be a positive person – someone you'd *want* to spend time with and be friends with.

Someone who:

- you can talk to if you're worried
- values your opinion
- makes you laugh and who you can have fun with
- introduces you to new ideas, interests, or new people, who shares their time, ideas, or resources
- you can be inspired by
- challenges you to see the world in a new way.

The positive people in your life do not just have to be friends or family; they could be colleagues or neighbours. The person you could talk to if you were worried or you could call on in a crisis could be your GP, a support worker, or a therapist. The people who appreciate you could be people you help through some voluntary work that you do. Maybe the person who introduces you to new ideas and interests is an author or a teacher. Perhaps there's someone on the radio or TV who makes you laugh. The person who inspires you could be someone you've read about who has overcome adversity or who has achieved something despite all the odds.

Surround yourself with people who make you happy. People who make you laugh, who help you when you're in need. People who genuinely care. They are the ones worth keeping in your life. Everyone else is just passing through.

Karl Marx

Top Tip

Be the Friend You Would Like to Have

Get in touch with someone when you know they're going through a difficult time. Phone or send them a card, email, or text; cook a meal or send flowers or some other thoughtful expression to let them know you care and are thinking about them.

In a nutshell

- To develop close friendships you need to be prepared to open up yourself and be open to others.
- You don't have to reveal your deepest hopes, thoughts, and fears but you do need to share something that's a bit more personal than you might normally share.
- Be honest and sincere; talk about what you think and how you feel about things.

- If the other person readily offers their thoughts, ideas, and understanding you can feel encouraged that you've started to make a closer connection.
- Be careful not to use confiding in others and over-disclosing too early as a strategy to endear yourself to someone. It could come off as needy.
- Tell the other person your goals and what's going well, too. Tell them something you've learnt about yourself, about others, or your interactions with other people.
- Do they seem interested? Do they ask you questions about you, as if they'd like to get to know you better? Do they tell you things about themselves?
- Ask people about themselves. Find out what they've achieved and what challenges they've overcome. Ask what they feel and think about things.
- If the other person doesn't seem interested in what you have to say or they're not forthcoming with talking about themselves, that's OK. Everyone has their limits; maybe, for whatever reason, they won't or can't provide the interest and closeness that you're seeking.
- Be careful not to misunderstand or misinterpret the attention of others; you may make yourself vulnerable to those whose motives are not genuine and sincere; people who aren't good for you.

- Catfishing scammers take advantage of people looking for romantic partners on dating web sites, apps, or social media. They look to build relationships for the sole purpose of getting another person's money and/or their personally identifiable information.
- It's not just romance scammers that aren't good for you. A negative relationship with a friend, colleague, or family member can also be harmful and leave you feeling isolated and lonely.
- Be aware of the effect a 'drain's' negativity is having on you and, as much as possible, reduce the amount of time you spend around them and increase the amount of time you spend with radiators, the positive people you know.
- When looking to make new friends, you're looking for positive people! People who you can be yourself with, who make you feel good about yourself; who listen to you and encourage you.

9
Managing Existential Loneliness

Everybody hurts
Don't throw your hand
Oh, no
Don't throw your hand
If you feel like you're alone
No, no, no, you're not alone
W. Berry / P. Buck / M. E. Mills / J. Stipe

Existential loneliness happens when you are feeling entirely separate and disconnected from other people as a result of a difficult, challenging, or traumatic experience. It could be a situation that you're currently going though or something that happened in the past.

Distressing, frightening events such as experiencing or witnessing a terrorist attack; an accident, injury, or assault; being burgled or robbed; a natural or manmade disaster – situations where there was risk of or actual harm, danger, or death for yourself or other people – are all traumatic experiences which can knock you sideways.

As well as specific events, trauma can also happen as a result of a prolonged experience such as a serious chronic health problem, domestic or sexual abuse, or homelessness. So can caring long term for someone else – a friend, a child, your partner, a sibling or parent – with a physical or mental illness, or coping with your own physical or mental illness.

Trauma can also be the result of losing something or someone you love – a bereavement or a relationship break-up, losing your home or your job – incidents of discrimination, being harassed or bullied.

Whatever the issue and the circumstances, experiencing a trauma can leave you feeling, amongst other things, disconnected: lonely, anxious, and vulnerable.

You probably feel that no one understands what you experienced at the time and that they can't or won't even try to understand how you're feeling now. As a result, you might withdraw from family and friends or simply find it difficult to relate to or trust others.

As the author C. S. Lewis noted after the death of his wife: 'There is a sort of invisible blanket between the world and me. I find it hard to take in what anyone says.'

Reliving the trauma over and over again might also cause you to withdraw from others because the world feels unsafe. It could be that family and friends do want to understand and help but they're unsure *how* to be supportive.

Loneliness can also be exacerbated when whatever led to the trauma took place because you were already lonely or socially isolated. Perhaps, for example, you became the victim of an online dating scam (see Chapter 8, pages 113–116 for more on this). Others might think you've been foolish and gullible – easily deceived and cheated – and the ongoing shame, embarrassment, and self-blame you experience has left you feeling even more isolated and alone.

Writing About Your Experience

Although talking to trusted friends and family can help you feel less alone, for one reason or another, you might find it too difficult to explain what happened and how you're feeling. Writing about it can be a good first step and lead to talking and reaching out to others for support.

If you're currently experiencing difficulties and challenges, you could journal: regularly write down your thoughts and feelings. That might be every day or every few days. Doing this can help you to organize your thoughts and feelings. So can writing about a situation *after* it's happened; it can help your mind to break free of the endless going over and over and reliving the event.

A note of caution though: writing about a traumatic event, even one that happened some time ago, could trigger some difficult thoughts and feelings which might overwhelm you. Do be aware of where you can get professional help and support – pages 133–144 and pages 210–214 have information about organizations that can help.

Post-Traumatic Stress Disorder

Whilst some people who are exposed to trauma can move on from it, for others it's not that simple. Trauma can leave ongoing symptoms that need professional support and psychotherapeutic intervention.

On the UK's National Health Service's website www .nhs.uk/ the NHS suggests that it's 'normal to experience upsetting and confusing thoughts after a traumatic event, but most people improve naturally over a few weeks. You should see your doctor if you are still having problems about 4 weeks after the traumatic experience.'

The Royal College of Psychiatrists agrees www .rcpsych.ac.uk/ On their website page titled *Coping After a Traumatic Event* they explain that you should see your GP if difficult thoughts and feelings are too much for you, or go on for too long; if you experience some or all of the following:

- you have nightmares and cannot sleep
- you have no one to share your feelings with
- you are getting on badly with those close to you
- you stay away from other people more and more
- your work is suffering

- those around you suggest you seek help
- you are drinking or smoking too much, or using drugs to cope with your feelings

The RCP goes on to say: 'Traumatic events can be very difficult to come to terms with, but confronting your feelings and seeking professional help is often the only way of effectively treating Post-Traumatic Stress Disorder. It *is* possible for PTSD to be successfully treated many years after the traumatic event or events occurred, which means it's never too late to seek help.'

The Loneliness of Bereavement

In November 2019, comedian and artist Michael Kruz Kayne's posts on Twitter observed an aspect of grief and trauma that, he suggested, is often overlooked: loneliness. 'Grief is isolating, but not just because of the sadness. Also because the sadness is the only part about it that anyone knows ... having just recently started talking to other grievers, I know many of them feel the same.'

Donna Butler, a psychotherapist in Brighton, England, agrees. She says that in her work as a trauma psychotherapist, loneliness and isolation are experiences that her clients report, almost without exception. 'Existential loneliness can run a parallel path with those individuals who have experienced trauma and especially when it has resulted in the loss of a loved one. Even when clients have family or friends around them, there can be a sense of disconnection.'

The loss of a loved one – either as the result of a bereavement or relationship break-up – can bring an overwhelming sense of loneliness. You may have shared so much of your lives that the absence of that person's presence in your life leaves a big hole. You might miss the daily routines and interactions: the messages, the shared meals, watching TV together.

As the journalist Felicity Green has said: 'I have plenty of people to do things with, I just have no one to do nothing with.'

The Empty Chair

In an interview on BBC Radio 2's *Good Morning* show in October 2020, illustrator Gary Andrews described how, after the death of his wife, Joy, he changed where he sat in the living room. 'I sat in my wife's chair so I wouldn't have to look at her empty chair.'

As well as the daily interactions, you may miss the good times you shared together: the holidays, day trips, and meals out. You probably miss the celebrations – the birthdays and anniversaries – and family occasions – births, graduations, etc. – with someone who is invested in those events as much as you are. Other times, you can miss having that person to share concerns and the mutual support and encouragement you got from each other.

Some of your friends and family may have related to you as a couple. Feelings of loneliness can be compounded when they don't accommodate the fact that you are now single; there's no ill-will on their part, but they gradually stop inviting you to the sort of activities and events you used to be part of when your partner was there.

The Loneliness of Grief

Talking about grief and bereavement on BBC Radio 4's *Saturday Live* programme in January 2021, Rev. Richard Coles described how, knowing that his partner David had recently died, a woman came up to him in the street, took his hand and after expressing her condolences, said 'no one will ever be as nice to you as they are now'.

It's true; after a bereavement people *are* nice. But that can soon pass as they continue with their lives.

In an article in the *Guardian* newspaper in April 2019, Vanessa Billy described how, after her father died, in the weeks following his death people offered condolences and gave her space; her work colleagues were supportive, providing back-up, patience, and flexibility. A couple of months later, though, Vanessa says: 'I still had uncontrollable fits of crying or sadness, only met by uncomfortable silence and awkward looks around me ... Many times, I felt like watching the train I was supposed to be on depart while I stayed stuck on the platform.'

Vanessa did try to get back to her 'normal' self. She tried socializing but found it difficult to handle simple conversations. 'Increasingly, I started noticing people's uneasiness if I mentioned how I felt or the memories of my father. I now know that their embarrassment came from not knowing how to react.

'I knew grief was going to be painful. What I didn't know was how lonely it would make me feel.'

After a couple of months, Vanessa started to see a grief counsellor. 'This decision gave me my life back. The counsellor simply provided me with the space I needed to grieve. We spoke about my dad, about his last days, I cried a lot. Simply talking about it with someone who told me all this was normal gave me immense relief.'

Help and Support

Professional help and/or a support group – talking to people who are experiencing or have gone through similar situations – can provide a safe place to share, be listened to, get advice, support, and information.

You can connect with others via phone, video, email, or in person.

Below are just some of the organizations that can be of help. Whatever you've experienced – a bereavement, abuse, racism, a physical attack, harassment, being stalked, unfair loss of your job, an accident or illness – there *will* be support there for you. You've just got to make the first move.

Bereavement

CRUSE www.cruse.org.uk/ provides support and information for people who have experienced bereavement. Their helpline number is 0808 808 1677.

Just B https://justb.org.uk/ offer emotional wellbeing, bereavement, and trauma support nationally to NHS, care sector staff, and emergency service workers. Available seven days a week, 8am–8pm, by calling 0300 303 4434.

The Good Grief Project www.thegoodgriefproject.co .uk/ supports families grieving after the untimely death of a loved one, particularly the death of a child. They recognize what it means to grieve in a society that often has difficulty talking openly about death, dying, and bereavement.

Child Bereavement UK www.childbereavementuk.org/ helps children and young people (up to age 25), parents, and families, to rebuild their lives when a child grieves or when a child dies.

Tommy's www.tommys.org/ fund research into miscarriage, stillbirth, and premature birth. Tommy's recognize that some women – and/or their partners – find themselves feeling alone in their grief because nobody knew they were pregnant in the first place. They recognize that it can also be difficult if other people's reactions to your loss are unhelpful or upsetting.

Crime

Victim Support www.victimsupport.org.uk/ provides specialist practical and emotional support to victims and witnesses of crime. Their support line – 08 08 16 89 111 – operates 24/7.

Rape Crisis. On their website https://rapecrisis.org.uk/, Rape Crisis – who provide a range of services for women and girls who have experienced abuse, domestic violence, and sexual assault – recognize that amongst other things you're struggling with, you might feel isolated and alone, like you're the only person who's ever been through this or like you're different from everyone else. They say that 'whatever you do or don't feel now or in the future is OK, and talking to Rape Crisis can help'.

Over half their member Rape Crisis Centres provide specific support services for men and boys who have experienced sexual violence as a child and/or as an adult.

Being stalked. If you're worried that someone is stalking you, Suzy Lamplugh www.suzylamplugh.org Trust understand that it can feel difficult seeking support. But they *can* help.

The Loneliness of Domestic Abuse

On their website, the Women's Centre, in Michigan USA https://wcmqt.org/ state that 'the loneliness of abuse starts at the earliest stages of a relationship. Abusers isolate their victims, not just physically, but emotionally. People who suffer from abusive situations believe they are alone because the ... abuser ... tells them they are.

The seeds of isolation tend to start in the beginning, where an eventual abuser criticizes friends and family. Victims in this stage often feel pressure, even if it's emotional rather than physical, to disassociate from other people who love them. By the time physical or more severe emotional abuse begins, victims feel too disconnected from other relationships to tell anyone what's happening ... [they are] too ashamed to talk about it. That shame is isolating.

But it's not the only shame victims of abuse must overcome. People who try to help victims inadvertently isolate them by suggesting that they are 'better than that.' Victims interpret this as, "if I'm better than that but can't leave, then something must be wrong with me." Other times, friends may say "how could you let him/her do this to you," making it difficult for victims to ask for help. Advocates and allies mean well, but victim-blaming is another isolating factor for those suffering from domestic violence.'

> Staying silent and telling no one will only isolate you while at the same time empowering the abuser so you must get help and support. Don't be afraid to do this. There are people who can give you support and advice. There are organizations that specialize in supporting anyone who is being bullied or abused. In the UK, the national domestic abuse helpline www.nationaldahelpline.org.uk/ and Women's Aid www.womensaid.org.uk/ are two organizations that can help.

Whistle blowing. As research director at Second Chance Body Armor (since liquidated), Aaron Westrick urged his employer to recall a line of defective bulletproof vests containing Zylon, a material manufactured by Japanese company Toyobo. However, Aaron was not just ignored but frozen out. He was told by an HR officer, accompanied by his employer's attorney, that he was 'crazy'. He was sacked and maligned. 'If there's one word that describes being a whistleblower, it's loneliness,' he says. 'Even your friends don't really get it.'

If you've seen, heard, or suspect wrongdoing in your workplace, or know of a serious risk or accident 'waiting to happen' contact Protect www.protect-advice.org.uk/.

Get the Help and Support You Need

As you can see from the organizations listed in the last few pages, there's plenty of support, help, and advice available if you have suffered a bereavement or been on the receiving end of a crime. But these are not the only support organisations – whatever difficulty or trauma you have or you are experiencing, there *is* help available; there *will* be support there for you. You might have to be persistent and find the support that's right for you, but you've got to make the first move.

Google a relevant support group and/or helpline. You'll be able to talk to people who understand what you're going through, provide opportunities to share experiences, and information or ideas on how to move on or feel better.

It might be, though, that you think asking for help is a sign of weakness; you don't want anyone to see that you're struggling. You want people to think that you're in control and can handle things.

But you get in your own way when you make asking for help mean something negative about you when it doesn't. Asking for help doesn't mean you're inadequate, it simply means you need help, support and advice with a specific issue for a time.

Whatever the reason for you feeling lonely – alone and isolated – loneliness can lead to suicidal feelings. If you are experiencing suicidal thoughts and feelings, the Samaritans www.samaritans.org/ provide emotional support to anyone in emotional distress, struggling to cope, or at risk of suicide. Phone 116 123 or email jo@samaritans.org/ Please don't struggle on your own. Do call or email them.

Support Groups

It can be tough to talk to others about a trauma if they have no understanding of what it feels like to go through it. Joining a support group in real life or online can provide a place to share your feelings in a safe space, to feel validated and listened to. You can get a real sense of connection – feeling that you belong, and are with people who understand you.

Support groups may be organized by their members, or be facilitated by professionals. They may be groups that meet on a regular basis, or they may be an online community; they may be both.

Some support groups provide ongoing support for a past trauma, where the focus is on helping those involved to overcome or move beyond their experience. Others address persistent, long-lasting difficulties, with an emphasis on helping people to manage and cope with their situation.

In all cases, good support groups provide members with various forms of help, providing opportunities to share experiences and sensitive personal details, explaining how to find and use information, sharing or evaluating relevant research and information, providing empathy, and developing social networks.

Find Positivity

It's not easy to manage each day when you know you will be experiencing pain and sadness. So every day, decide to have something to look forward to. No matter how small it is, have something you can do that you enjoy and brings you small comforts.

Describing, in the newspaper *The Observer*, a hospital stay for IV fluids and a blood transfusion over Easter 2020, Sarah Hughes, who had a diagnosis of terminal cancer wrote: 'It is hard to describe how very lonely it feels to lie in a hospital bed with only the disease that will kill you for company.'

Sarah said that the only piece of advice she felt she could give is this: 'Try to find some part of the day that is worth relishing whether it is a moment of beauty half-glimpsed outside, the joy found in escaping into a different world on page or screen, or the pleasure of dressing up for yourself and no one else because it makes you feel fine.'

Post-Traumatic Growth

Research has found that trauma can be a powerful force for positive change. In the 1990s, University of North Carolina Professors Tedeschi and Calhoun discovered that more than half of the trauma survivors they interviewed reported positive change; they believed that their lives had eventually changed for the better. They had experienced what Tedeschi and Calhoun described as 'post-traumatic growth'.

Amongst other things, the people who had experienced trauma in Tedeschi and Calhoun's study felt that they had become wiser, stronger, more empathic and accepting of others, developed closer relationships, and now had more compassion for others. Many had re-evaluated their priorities, had a greater appreciation for things in their life, identified new possibilities, and often become more spiritual.

Reflect on the positive. If you've experienced a traumatic event it may help to think about what you've learnt about yourself, other people, and your place in the world:

- What inner strengths did you discover and draw on?
- Has your experience given you an empathy and understanding for other people when they are faced with adversity?
- How might you use what you've experienced and learnt to help yourself and other people or create something of personal or social value?
- What might you do differently – what new opportunities might there now be? What new relationships?
- How might you interact with people differently?

Whatever the issue and the circumstances, experiencing a trauma can leave you feeling disconnected: scared, anxious, and vulnerable. But it *can* also be the catalyst for positive change.

In a nutshell

- Existential loneliness happens when you are feeling entirely disconnected from other people as a result of a traumatic experience. It could be a situation that you're currently going though or something that happened in the past.
- Trauma can leave you feeling, amongst other things, lonely, anxious, and vulnerable, that no one understands. As a result, you might withdraw from others; you might find it difficult to relate to or trust others.
- Loneliness can also be exacerbated when whatever led to the trauma took place because you were already lonely or socially isolated. Others might think you've been foolish and gullible – easily deceived and cheated – and the ongoing shame, embarrassment and self-blame has left you feeling even more isolated and alone.
- Writing about your experience can help you to organize your thoughts and feelings. It can help your mind to break free from the endless going over and over and reliving the event. It can also lead to talking and reaching out to others for support.

- Writing about a traumatic event – one that you're currently going through or that happened some time ago – could trigger some difficult thoughts and feelings which might overwhelm you. Do be aware of where you can get professional help and support.
- Professional help and/or a support group can provide a safe place to share, be listened to, get advice, support, and information. You can connect with others via phone, video, email, or in person.
- Whatever trauma you've experienced there *will* be support there for you. You've just got to make the first move and be persistent in finding the support that's right for you.
- You get in your own way if you think that asking for help is a sign of weakness. Asking for help doesn't mean you're inadequate, it simply means you need help, support, and advice with a specific issue for a time.
- Research has found that trauma can be a powerful force for positive change. For many trauma survivors the experience led to positive change: 'post-traumatic growth'.
- Reflect on the positive. If you've experienced a traumatic event it may help to think what positive things you've learnt about yourself, other people, and your place in the world.

10
Spending Time Alone

What a lovely surprise to finally discover how unlonely being alone can be.

Ellen Burstyn

In his book *Solitude*, psychiatrist Dr Anthony Storr challenges the idea that interpersonal relationships are the key to feeling connected.

Whilst acknowledging the importance of friendship and love – the natural desire and need for positive relationships with other people – Dr Storr says 'they are not the only source of happiness ... [they are] a hub around which a person's life revolves, not necessarily *the* hub. The desire and pursuit of the whole (the striving for unity in life) must, he says, 'comprehend both aspects of human nature'.

The aspects of human nature that Storr is referring to are the same as those identified 2000 years ago by Aristotle in his *Nicomachean Ethics*. Aristotle also concluded that the perfect life required time for contemplation as well as friendship.

In other words, if we each want to feel happy and fulfilled, we need time with other people and we need time alone. We need solitude.

Storr says that solitude enables us to get in touch with our deepest feelings: 'to come to terms with loss; to sort out ... ideas; to change attitudes ... [to] encourage the growth of the creative imagination'. Storr recognizes, though, that imagination can be a problem. He points out: 'Imagination has given man flexibility; but in doing so, has robbed him of contentment.'

It's true; although we need time alone to think – to reflect and to plan ahead – too much time alone can lead at one extreme, to rumination, and at the other extreme, worry and anxiety. As the German philosopher Nietzsche said: 'It is what one takes into solitude that grows there, the beast within included.'

Certainly, being alone and not wanting to be alone too often or for long periods can be a real struggle. It's lonely. Loneliness is uncomfortable at best, downright miserable at worst. Solitude, on the other hand – being alone by choice – is comfortable. It's enjoying time alone; time away from other people.

Although it's completely normal to want to connect with and spend time with others, it's also important to feel at ease *without* others; to be comfortable and enjoy *some* time alone.

Being alone is about balance. Not being sad and not being happy about being in your own company but just being still and just being quiet, in balance. It has positive connotations to me.

Poorna Bell

As well as giving you time and space to think – to reflect and plan – solitude gives you time to process experience, to learn and assimilate learning. Time alone – solitude – is time that can be spent on interests, hobbies, and creative pursuits.

We put in an extraordinary amount of time teaching children to be sociable. Meanwhile we give them no training or support in the apparently difficult ... skill of being alone.

Sara Maitland

Instead of getting stuck in feelings of loneliness, look for ways to make time on your own easier. How? By doing things that you enjoy and make you feel good.

As the philosopher Jean-Paul Sartre said: 'If you're lonely when you're alone, you're in bad company.' So, you have to work at developing yourself into being someone whose company you're comfortable with, that you enjoy.

Find 'Flow'

Think about the times – even short periods of time – when you are on your own but you *don't* feel lonely; you're so absorbed in what you were doing that time passes without you realizing. What's happening? What are you doing during those periods? What's capturing your interest then?

Perhaps you're reading, listening to music, the radio, a podcast or audio book, or watching TV. Perhaps it's a musical instrument or a video game you're playing. Maybe you're gardening, doing something that involves arts and crafts.

Whatever it is, as you do it, no other thoughts enter your mind because you are completely focused and engaged in what you're doing; you don't even notice the time passing.

When you're doing something that keeps you effortlessly focused and engaged like this, you're experiencing some-thing known as 'flow'. When you're in a state of flow, it's as if a water current is effortlessly carrying you along. Your awareness merges with what you're doing and you are completely 'in the moment'. Your thoughts are pos-itive and in tune with what you're doing.

What do you like doing? What activities can you engage with for half an hour – a crossword, a jigsaw, or sudoku – or immerse yourself in for an hour or more – Swimming? Running? Fishing? Maybe you enjoy cooking?

Identify the things you enjoy doing; hobbies, sports, interests. Know that when you have time alone, they are activities where you can easily experience flow. Hobbies and creative interests can be an important source of connection and provide stability and contentment.

When you're involved in an activity that gives you a sense of flow, you're doing something that's meaningful; there's a purpose and an aim to what you're doing. Even though there may be an element of challenge – such as a puzzle, a game, or learning something new – it's enjoyable, there's progression, and it maintains your interest. You feel connected and content.

Do Something!

There are plenty of activities you can do that will give you a sense of flow. Here are some that cost very little or are free.

Books and films. It could be a gripping thriller, science fiction, or a clever comedy. Whatever the genre, as events unfold, you become lost in the story.

At your local library, you can borrow books for free, including graphic novels and books in other languages. You can also borrow music scores for free, a range of e-books and e-audiobooks. DVDs, CDs, audiobooks, and language courses are available to borrow for a small fee. Charity shops are also good for books, audiobooks, DVDs, and CDs.

I never feel lonely if I've got a book, they're like old friends. Even if you're not reading them over and over again, you know they are there.

Emilia Fox

Learn a language. You can sign up to a class but you can also learn on your own, for free. Go to Duolingo: www .duolingo.com/ As the Duolingo strapline says; 'Learn a language for free. Forever.'

Writing. If you can read, you can write. Try poems or short stories. Try writing stories for children. Keep a journal, write your life story, start a blog.

Cooking. You've got to eat. You're going to spend money on food anyway. You could use it as an opportunity to learn new recipes. Go to www.bbc.co.uk/food/ for a wide range of recipes.

Bird-watching. The RSPB says: 'You don't need much to enjoy birds – just your eyes or ears. But there are lots of things which can make it easier or more enjoyable. We have advice on buying the right kit to help you get off to a great start.' www.rspb.org.uk/

Get creative. We all have the ability to be creative. Whether it's doodling, drawing or painting, embroidery, sculpture, cake decorating, calligraphy, origami, or one of dozens of different art and craft activities, doing something creative can be a positive way of being focused and engaged.

What art activities might you like doing? Sketching, clay modelling, scrapbooking? Know that when you need to bring together your mind, body, and environment, arts and crafts are activities where you can easily experience flow.

Drawing. All you need is some paper and a pencil. But what if you've got no artistic talent? Illustrator and portrait painter Gilly Lovegrove www.gillylovegroveillus tration.com/ says that, 'with the right tuition/guidance, a positive attitude and allowing time to the subject, anyone can learn to draw'.

Photography. There's no need to buy an expensive camera; assuming you've already got a phone with a camera, brilliant results can be obtained with a camera phone.

For both drawing and photography you'll find instructional videos on YouTube. www.youtube.co.uk/

Music and dance. Listening to or playing music, singing, and dancing can also provide a sense of flow. Music, singing, and dancing can provide a focus that ranges from being totally energizing to calming and relaxing. Make a playlist of songs that uplift you. Sing out loud and dance like no one's watching.

It's almost impossible to feel lonely when you're singing. I've tried it, and it works. Sing solo or let your favorite singer keep you company as you sing together.

Toni Bernhard

As with art, music and dancing can be different languages to express how you feel. Make your own music; if you don't already know how, learn to play an instrument; it's never too late!

Top Tip

Plan Ahead

A good idea is to identify, in advance, the times and occasions when you might feel loneliness more acutely – more intensely. Make a list of activities and interests that you can 'lose yourself' in, whether it's for half an hour, a few hours, or a weekend. Doing things that you enjoy can help you move through lonely periods.

Small Pleasures and Awesome Things

As well as activities that engage you for a few hours, there's a world of small pleasures which can bring you moments of connection and happiness every day. We all have things that we enjoy, that give us pleasure and moments of happiness.

What, for you, makes for small pleasures? A bubble bath or a hot shower? A cup of tea of coffee? Maybe it's a perfectly ripe peach or pear. Perhaps it's an open fire, sitting in the sun, or a walk in the rain? Maybe talking to your dog or cat is one of your small pleasures. Whatever they may be, indulge in them more often!

Explore New Activities and Hobbies

Don't be afraid to try new things. New experiences give you something to talk about which will interest and connect you to other people. You will also be able to reach out to others with less of a need and more of an ability to give. You will find you have more interest in other people and the world around you.

Practised solitude increases self-knowledge and independence. And this makes us less vulnerable to emotional abuse and more able to remove ourselves from such situations. And this in itself may well make us a better, because less needy, friend when we do engage.

Sara Maitland

Home Study

- Open University (OU) open.ac.uk/ offers more than degrees. Their Short Courses programme is for those people who want to study entirely online for personal interest or professional development. The OU also has a wide range of free courses www.open.edu/openlearn/free-courses/full-catalogue/ covering, for example, Nature and the Environment, Health Sports and Psychology, and History and the Arts. Courses range from a three-hour class titled 'Janis Joplin and the Sexual Revolution' to a 16-hour course on 'Napoleonic Paintings' and a 24-hour course 'The Science of Nutrition and Healthy Eating'.

- Future Learn futurelearn.com/ allow you to learn online with world-class universities and industry experts. They are for people who want to develop their career, learn a new skill, or pursue a specific interest or hobby. A wide range of Future Learn's courses are free.

If you have a hobby or interest that you can lose yourself in, you will find yourself actually searching out time to be by yourself in order to do what you enjoy. Whatever the activity you choose, you'll know that periods of time spent alone can be rewarding; they can help you to feel engaged and connected. You can relax and accept a calmer sense of yourself.

Do Something from Home, for Other People

Spending some time doing something for someone else will not only give you something to do, it will also give you a real sense of purpose and connection. Here are a few ideas:

1. Map a disaster zone www.missingmaps.org/
   Help make maps to inform the relief efforts of organizations such as the Red Cross with Missing Maps. Volunteers use satellite images and a drawing tool to mark up buildings, rivers, and roads in remote areas that may not have been mapped before. This helps organizations who are first to respond make more informed decisions about disaster relief.

2. Knit or sew a book bag www.bagbooks.org/

   Bag Books is a UK-registered charity supporting people with learning disabilities through the provision of multisensory books and storytelling. They need home-based sewing and knitting volunteers.

3. Help a child to read www.bookmarkreading.org/

   As a Bookmark online volunteer, you'll help a 5–8-year-old learn to read so that they can succeed in school. The two 30-minute virtual reading sessions each week (which you arrange for a time to suit you and the child) include reading, and fun interactive word games and activities with a child.

4. Expose biases https://implicit.harvard.edu/implicit/

   Project Implicit researchers investigate the subconscious way our minds work. Volunteers take psychological tests online to help researchers better understand society's hidden biases and prejudices and how we might tackle them.

5. Improve disabled access www.axsmap.com/

   Help make your neighbourhood more accessible by ranking shops and restaurants for their disabled-friendly credentials. Enter your postcode on the AXS Map website to bring up a map and list of businesses. You can then rate these using a star system and also leave reviews.

6. Lend someone your vision www.bemyeyes.com/

   Using the Be My Eyes app, virtual volunteers can help a blind or low-vision person to go about their daily tasks. Through a live video call, you can help to solve problems like checking expiry dates, distinguishing colours, reading instructions, or navigating new surroundings.

7. Watch the birds https://ebird.org/home/

   Track your bird sightings via the eBird website and become part of a worldwide network of birdwatchers. Your sightings contribute to hundreds of conservation decisions and help inform global bird research. And you can explore birds and hotspots near you with dynamic maps that chart every species in the world.

8. Help expose human rights violations https://decoders .amnesty.org/

   Amnesty Decoder volunteers use their computers or phones to help Amnesty researchers sift through pictures, information, and documents to help expose human rights violations. Projects that volunteers have helped to decode include making oil companies accountable for devastating oil pollution in Nigeria, identifying Darfur's most remote villages, and exposing abuse that silences women on #ToxicTwitter.

Top Tip

Do Something Nice

Make, bake, or cook something for someone else. Then deliver it to them in person or send it to them.

Going Out Alone

It's interesting that many of us don't mind going out and doing routine chores and activities alone – going to the supermarket, for example, or the bank, or the dentist.

But we're uncomfortable – even embarrassed – about doing enjoyable leisure activities by ourselves. We don't think we'd like watching a movie, dining out, going to the cinema, theatre, a concert, exhibition, or some other event by ourselves. Certainly, it is good and enjoyable to share activities, and thoughts and opinions about activities, with others. But there is value in going out and doing things alone. Worried about what others might think? Don't be worried. As Eleanor Roosevelt once said: 'You wouldn't worry so much about what others think of you if you realized how seldom they do.'

Francesca Specter is the author of *Alonement: How To Be Alone and Absolutely Own It* and has a podcast www.alonement.com/alonement-podcast/ where she interviews others about the positive aspects of spending time alone.

Francesca's advice to others would be to choose somewhere small to start with and then just go for it. 'I started out just by going to the cinema. I think once you realize that you are in a big dark room where no one else can see you, you don't feel judged and you don't necessarily feel like anyone is watching you. From there, you can build out into whatever else you want to do.'

Get Out in Nature

A 2019 study by the University of Exeter Medical School has found that people who spend at least 120 minutes each week in nature are significantly more likely to report good health and higher psychological wellbeing than those who don't. The study reports that it doesn't matter whether the 120 minutes was achieved in a single visit or over several shorter visits.

Try and organize your days so that you can spend time in nature. Most people have somewhere near them, even if it's only a small park or garden. With more than 62,000 urban green spaces in Great Britain, one should never be too far away. The Wildlife Trusts www .wildlifetrusts.org/ have a searchable online map of their nature reserves, almost all of which have free entry; they also provide a list of accessible nature reserves. And Ordnance Survey's Greenspace – getoutside.ordnance survey.co.uk/greenspaces/ shows thousands of green spaces for leisure and recreation.

Spend time with animals. Time spent with a pet – a cat, dog, or other pet animal – can be calming and comforting, providing an unconditional exchange of care and love.

If you'd like to spend time with an animal but don't have your own, organizations like BorrowMyDoggy borrow mydoggy.com connect dog owners with others who would like to walk or dog-sit and share the care of a dog.

Find Spirituality

Spirituality is a sense of being connected and part of something bigger, more eternal than both yourself and the physical world.

For many people, a spiritual life is to be found through their religious beliefs: the connection to a higher being, the rituals, prayers, meditations, or mantras involved. Although spirituality can be part of a religion, it can also be seen as being distinct from religion. You don't have to be religious in order to be spiritual. Even if you regard yourself as an agnostic or atheist, you can feel a sense of connection to something larger and more everlasting than yourself. You can choose to define what spirituality means for you in whatever way feels most appropriate.

Your own sense of spirituality might come from something as simple as the power of the ocean, the beauty of the sunset, or the enormity of a star-filled sky. Concepts such as beauty, music and creativity, imagination and peace, and the miracles of nature can all contribute to a sense of spirituality – to connecting with something profound, no matter how simple or awesome.

Spirituality helps you to feel grounded in the present and yet connected to the past and the future. People who are separated from their cultures, for example, may find that their shared spiritual beliefs and practices provide connections with their cultural identity.

Think about what you already do that makes you feel connected. Perhaps it's playing a team sport, singing in a choir, gardening or being outside with nature, or being with thousands of others at a music festival. Get connected. Appreciate the beauty of which we are naturally a part, concepts such as music and art, wildlife, and the miracles of nature.

Top Tip

Manage the Loneliness of Sleeplessness

'In my experience, when you can't sleep and it's the middle of the night, it feels lonely', says Drew Ackerman, Drew's popular Sleep With Me podcast www.sleepwithmepodcast.com/ lulls listeners to sleep with bedtime stories. While originally created for insomniacs, he found a wide and unexpected audience in lonely individuals. Thanks to his podcast, listeners fall asleep feeling like they have Drew right by their side.

Appreciate Three Things

However you've spent time on your own, at the end of each day write down three good things that have happened that day. Just make an effort for a couple of weeks to identify the good things – the small pleasures – in your day. After a while, identifying and reflecting on the small pleasures will become a habit. A happiness habit.

Perhaps you had a good hair day. Your favourite song came on the radio at the perfect moment. Or you ate a perfectly ripe avocado. Maybe something arrived that you forgot you'd ordered online. Or you managed to fix something like a cupboard door or undo a knot in a shoelace. Maybe you dropped your phone, thought the screen had smashed, but then realized it hadn't. Or it could be that you arrived late to meet someone only to find the other person was even later. Perhaps you received a humorous text from a friend or your dog did something that made you laugh.

I've been writing down three good things that have happened in my day, every day. It doesn't matter how big or small they are. It could be having pastries in bed. Spotting a fox in the garden. Successfully descaling a kettle ... I have found it vital ... to focus on the things that have gone right. Left unattended, my thoughts have a tendency to slip into a downward spiral.

Kathryn Bromwich

Even if you have a bad day, find three good things that happened. You could write them down in a notebook, or you may simply reflect on what those things are while you are brushing your teeth. Appreciate just realizing that you had good in your day so that, whatever else happened, you know that you did have things that made it worthwhile. Do this before you go to bed every night, and no matter what happened that day, you go to bed feeling OK.

In a nutshell

- Relationships are important but they're not the only way to feel connected. You need a balance; it's important to feel at ease without others; to be comfortable and enjoy some time alone.

- Solitude gives you time and space to think – to reflect and plan – to process experience, to learn and assimilate learning. Time alone can be spent on interests, hobbies, and creative pursuits.
- Instead of getting stuck in feelings of loneliness, look for ways to make time on your own easier. How? By doing things that you enjoy and make you feel good.
- Identify the things you enjoy doing: hobbies, sports, interests. You'll find yourself actually searching out time to be by yourself in order to do what you enjoy. You'll know that periods of time spent alone can be rewarding; they can help you to feel engaged and connected.
- Explore new activities and hobbies. New experiences give you something to talk about which will interest and connect you to other people.
- Doing something that benefits someone else will not only give you something to do, it will also give you a real sense of purpose and connection.
- As well as activities that engage you for a few hours, there's a world of small pleasures which can bring you moments of connection and happiness every day. Whatever your small pleasures, indulge in them more often!
- Go out alone; choose to do something that's a small step out of your comfort zone and then just go for it.
- Try and organize your days so that you spend some time in nature. Most people have

somewhere near them, even if it's only a small park or garden.

- Spend time with animals. Time spent with a pet – a cat, dog, or other pet animal – can be calming and comforting, providing an unconditional exchange of care and love.
- Find spirituality: a sense of being connected and part of something bigger, more eternal than both yourself and the physical world. Spirituality helps you to feel grounded in the present and yet connected to the past and the future.
- However you've spent your time, at the end of each day write down three good things that have happened that day.

11
Working from Home and Loneliness at Work

Things work out best for those who make the best of how things work out.

John Wooden

More and more people are working where they live and living where they work. Even before the coronavirus pandemic hit in 2020, in the UK there were already 4.8 million freelancers, mostly home-based workers, making up a significant 15% of the workforce, and companies were increasingly allowing employees to work remotely.

Like many people, you might be someone who enjoys working from home. The flexibility, not having to commute, having your space set up exactly how you want it, and being able to work in your pyjamas are just some of the benefits that come with working from home. So are not having a boss to stand over you and micromanage you, having coworkers constantly interrupt you, less involvement in office politics, taking a break when it suits you, being free to listen to music and podcasts while you work or have complete silence.

I look forward to my lunches, usually reheated leftovers but it's much better and less expensive than any of the cafes or sandwich bars I used to go to when I worked from an office in the middle of town. Eating alone doesn't bother me, I listen to the radio.

Jasper, an employee in a public relations company

But what if you don't like working from home? What if, for you, working on your own at home is isolating and lonely? For all of the benefits of not having to go into the office every day, there's also a downside: whole days can easily slip by when you don't go out or actually speak to another person.

The lack of social interaction and sense of belonging that come from working as part of a team can be hard to manage. Perhaps you miss the chats by the coffee machine, the lift, or on the stairs and having someone to go for lunch with and share ideas with. It is, after all, through those small interactions with colleagues that connections are made.

You may struggle to get help, advice, and support when you run into problems with your work. And, as well as the lack of interaction with colleagues, it may be that you find it harder to get motivated without other people around you. The proximity of the fridge and biscuit tin, lack of exercise, difficulty in setting boundaries between work and life outside work can also make working from home a difficulty and a challenge.

The Sound of Colleagues

In the summer of 2020, as the Covid pandemic continued to affect people's lives, more than half a million people tuned in to The Sound of Colleagues, a web page and Spotify playlist of workplace sounds, including keyboards, printers, chatter, and coffee machines. Red Pipe, a Swedish music and sound studio, created it in April that year as a joke, but its data suggested that people did actually keep it on in the background.

Get Connected. Stay Connected

There *are* ways to reduce isolation and get connected, perhaps boosting the wellbeing of colleagues as well as your own. You just have to be prepared to make the effort. Here are some ideas – a list of do's and don'ts – to help you:

- Do start online meetings by asking colleagues about their weekends or their families. Ask a random question – What's the last good book you read? What's the last good TV show or series you've watched? Podcasts you'd recommend? – or any of the questions on pages 86–88. When you're hardly ever in the same room, it's a way to get to know each other.

- Do ask how your colleagues feel about working from home. Discuss ways you could support each other.
- Do make time to socialize virtually; schedule in a digital coffee break or Friday online get-together.
- Do try to keep to a regular schedule and divide your day up into work, short breaks, meals, and physical activity.
- Don't skip lunch. Do take a proper lunchbreak. There are probably other people – neighbours, family, or friends – nearby who also work from home. Arrange to meet up with those people. Meet for a short walk, a sandwich in the park, a snack in a cafe or pub.
- Do make plans for after work too. Plans that involve meeting up with family and friends. As someone who works from home writing for large parts of the day, I rarely feel isolated because, a few days in the week, I meet up with a friend or neighbour for coffee, lunch, or a walk.
- Don't sit or stand still for long periods. You need to be more active; take frequent breaks that involve moving around.

Breaking up sitting time engages your muscles and bones, and gives all our bodily functions a boost – a bit like revving a car's engine.

Professor David Dunstan, Baker Heart and Diabetes Institute in Melbourne

---

- Don't just stick to video calls that keep you at your desk – pick up the phone instead and move around the room or stare out of a different window as you talk.
- Do look out the window. Notice the changes in the sky. Go back to the window often throughout the day and be aware of being connected to something bigger than the space you're confined to.

Keeping Social Contact – Five Stories

After working from home for two years as a freelance copywriter, Kieran found the lack of interaction with other people was getting him down. 'What made a big difference was when I decided to take time out one morning a week to volunteer at a local charity shop. I get on well with the other volunteers at the shop and the manager put me on the till so I could chat with and help customers. It made all the difference to my week.'

For Sam, adopting Ralph – a rescue dog – provided companionship and structure to Sam's working day. 'We go for a long walk first thing before I sit down at my desk and then again at 5pm. Not only do I get daily exercise but I usually run into other dog owners and a couple of neighbours and we have a quick a chat. And the late afternoon walk brings my work day to a natural close.'

During lockdown in the spring of 2020 and the winter of 2020/21, my husband and a few friends living in Brighton and London, each working from home, set up a daily album listening session. They use a timer app – https://liveclock.net/ – to synchronize the time at 5pm and then all listen to an album one of them had suggested earlier that day. As I write this, they're all listening to Mick Ronson's 'Slaughter on 10th Avenue'. Yesterday it was Aretha Franklin's Greatest Hits.

The loneliness that can come with working from home is one of the reasons that freelance editor Louise Goss launched the *Homeworker* magazine https://www .thehomeworker.com/. Beyond the articles on relevant resources, advice and support with self-assessment tax returns to desk-based Pilates, Louise's aim with the magazine is to foster a sense of community: 'Just that feeling that, even though you're on your own, you're not alone.'

During the 2020 winter lockdown, writer Tim Dowling had an amusing suggestion: order something small on a regular basis: 'a book, some seeds, 100 galvanized wood screws, insoles, replacement wheels for your upper dishwasher rack. The aim is to establish a steady rhythm, with a package arriving for you every day. Not only does this give you something to look forward to, it automatically triggers a daily doorstep social interaction, where a masked delivery person waves at you from a distance of 2 metres while pointing to the parcel at your feet. Sometimes, in my experience, they even take a picture.'

Lonely in the Workplace

You don't have to be working on your own at home for work to be lonely. Working with others can leave you feeling lonely and isolated too. Here's Lara's experience:

Four weeks into her new job, Lara would sit at her desk, watching the office fill up. Groups of people would chat about their weekends and exchange news over coffee as they settled down to work. Lara wanted to be part of these conversations, but no one invited her and she didn't feel able to approach the groups; she wasn't part of the 'in crowd'.

As each day wore on, Lara would try and focus on her work while at the same time trying to ignore feelings of being alone and isolated. By end of day, Lara was unhappy, feeling depressed and anxious. She didn't know what to do. Keep quiet and hope that things would get better? Ask HR for advice? Or, perhaps just call it quits and find another job somewhere else?

As the weeks progressed, Lara came to the conclusion that she just didn't fit in. And the reason she didn't fit in was because she was working in an area and with people whose values were very different to hers. So, Lara gave some thought to what her work values were – what was important to her in a job – and applied for jobs that were more in line with her true self. (Chapter 7 has more on values and fitting in.)

Of course, you're not always going to get on with everyone, but work politics can be a real challenge. So can having a difficult relationship with your colleagues or a manager; it can be stressful, and make work harder to manage. In fact, poor relationships at work can be really harmful when they are characterized by bullying and harassment.

Dealing with Bullying and Harassment

While the closely related concept of harassment is grounded in legal definition (in the Equality Act 2010 and other legislation) and has associated legal protections and recourse, there is no standard definition of what is considered to be an act of bullying. Ideas of what makes for bullying behaviour can vary widely according to context and the perceptions of the people involved: what may be considered, for example, reasonable behaviour by one person may be experienced as bullying by another. The options for resolution can also be unclear.

Bullying, as defined by ACAS, is 'offensive, intimidating, malicious or insulting behaviour, an abuse or misuse of power through means that undermine, humiliate, denigrate or injure the recipient'. Bullying can happen to anyone.

If you're being bullied then you may well feel very upset: lonely and isolated, anxious and frightened, ashamed or embarrassed. You may also feel angry and frustrated.

You mustn't try and pacify or ingratiate yourself with them, but you *must* do something. The bully will not go away. Staying silent and telling no one will only isolate you while at the same time empowering the bully, so you must get some help and support. Don't suffer in silence; there *is* help out there.

If you're not ready or feel unable to talk to someone at work about it, ACAS – the UK organization that provides impartial advice on workplace rights, rules, and best practice – have advice on their website www.acas.org.uk/ (search for Bullying and Harassment at Work – a Guide for Employees). ACAS also have a helpline that can provide you with advice on what to do if you're being bullied at work; you can find the phone number on their website. Citizens Advice www.citizensadvice.org.uk/ can also provide information and support. Go to their website and search for 'If you're being harassed or bullied at work'.

If you're being bullied and nothing changes for the better, or you do not feel as if you can take action, you may decide that leaving your job is the best option for your wellbeing and mental health.

By leaving, you regain control; you take away the opportunity for the bully to behave like this towards you. Being bullied and trying to manage being bullied is highly stressful. Ask yourself what's most important? Is it that you don't want to let the bully 'win'? Is that the most important issue? Rather than think in terms of one of you winning or losing, it's far better to think about keeping yourself safe and sane. Yes, you might have to walk away from a good job and financial stability, but focus on the positive; that you've left that person behind. Once you have left, you can put your energy into finding a new job instead of spending your energy trying to please, pacify, or avoid the bully.

If you do want to think in terms of who's won and who's lost – know that if you take control and walk away – you have won. You can manage to find a new job or somewhere to live. What you can't manage is the bully. So refuse to allow your life to be wrecked and get out!

Working at Home as a Carer

If you are one of the 7 million adults in the UK who look after a sick or disabled family member or friend you may have found that a lack of personal time, low income, and high levels of stress have left you, like so many other carers, feeling isolated and lonely.

Maybe you're unable to get out of the house much due to your caring responsibilities. Perhaps the only time you spend away from home and engage with someone is going shopping or to health appointments. Perhaps you don't have the time or the money to take part in hobbies and activities, where you would chat and interact with others.

You may have lost touch with family and friends as a result of your caring role. Even if you are in contact with others, it could be that you feel uncomfortable talking to them about your life as a carer. It could be that you don't feel able to freely express your thoughts and feelings; you fear you'll be judged, not understood, or misunderstood. And that would just increase your loneliness and isolation.

Carers UK Survey

In a 2014 survey of carers by the organization Carers UK, carers were asked what would help them feel less lonely. Of the respondents:

- 54% said regular breaks
- 29% said being in touch with other carers
- 21% said being able to take part in education or training opportunities
- 23% said being able to talk to family and friends
- 40% said being able to take part in leisure activities

Getting Support and Advice

Do make contact with others who already have a good understanding of how you are feeling, such as joining a forum just for carers. Carers UK recognize that caring can be very lonely. 'But,' they say 'you're not on your own. Carers UK is here to listen, to give you expert information and advice that's tailored to your situation, to champion your rights and support you in finding new ways to manage at home, at work, or wherever you are.'

There's also a wide range of support groups with forums and helplines covering specific illnesses and conditions such as dementia, and autism. The National Autistic Society's (www.autism.org.uk/) 'Parent to Parent' is a confidential telephone service providing emotional support to parents and carers of autistic adults or children. The service is provided by trained parent volunteers who are all parents of an autistic adult or child. The phone number is 0808 800 4106.

If you are a young carer – or know someone who is – Spurgeons Children's Charity https://spurgeons.org/ and Barnardo's offer a wide range of services to support young carers, from mentoring and educational support to activities and trips away to give them much needed time out from their caring duties.

The important thing to know is, that although it might not feel like it, you are not alone. But you will need to take that first step and reach out. Someone is there waiting to say 'hello'.

In a nutshell

- There are ways to reduce isolation if you are working from home. You have to be prepared to make the effort to keep connected. You also need to think outside the box; think creatively of ways to connect with and keep connected to other people during your working day.

- You don't have to be working on your own at home for work to be lonely. Working with others can leave you feeling isolated and lonely too.
- Poor relationships at work can be really harmful when they are characterized by bullying and harassment. You *must* do something. Staying silent and telling no one will only isolate you while at the same time empowering the bully, so you must get some help and support. Don't suffer in silence; there is help out there.
- As a carer looking after a sick or disabled family member or friend you may have found that a lack of personal time, low income, and high levels of stress have left you, like so many other carers, feeling isolated and lonely.
- Do make contact with others who already have a good understanding of how you are feeling. There's a wide range of support groups with forums and helplines that can help you. Do get in touch with them.

12
Being Inclusive: Helping Others to Connect and to Belong

In order to feel connected, we need to be seen, heard and valued.

Baya Voce

Be Welcoming, Approachable, and Inclusive

Can you remember a time when someone made a point of welcoming and including you – as a new employee, at someone's family occasion, a club, a meeting or conference, as a parent of young children at a toddler club, maybe on holiday, being welcomed into a local community celebration?

Whether it's welcoming friends and acquaintances into your home; customers, clients, or visitors to your workplace; or a new member to a club you belong to – it's important to treat people with kindness and respect; to make them feel welcome, that you're pleased they're there.

Being welcoming involves saying hello and saying you're pleased to see them or meet them. It's also about making them feel included and that they belong. Aim to be inclusive: to enable people to feel part of something; to feel that they can be involved in what you're doing or talking about.

If you're at a party or work event, introduce them to other people – people they may have something in common with. For example, you might introduce your sister to a colleague by saying, 'Ali, Josh has just come back from a trip to Italy. Josh, Ali lived in Italy for a couple of years.'

At work or in social situations, make a point of including people in a conversation so no one is left out. If someone isn't saying much in a group, ask them a specific question to bring them in. Don't draw attention to it by saying something like 'You're awfully quiet, Rosa', just say 'Rosa, what do you think about what we were just saying ... ?'

Supporting Someone Who Is Lonely

If you have a friend or relative who often experiences loneliness, do try and remember how you felt when you've been lonely; what went through your mind, how you felt emotionally and physically, what you did and what you didn't do. What helped and didn't help.

Reflecting on your experience of loneliness might help you to understand – to empathize with – how someone you know is feeling if they are struggling with loneliness. Don't though, assume that your experience of being lonely is necessarily the same as theirs. We all experience loneliness differently and we all think and feel and respond differently.

The important thing to know about empathy is that, actually, you might not 'get' it; you might not understand. And that's OK. You don't need to have experienced the same situation as they have, you don't have to agree that you'd feel the same way in the same situation, you just need to recognize the other person's feelings and emotions as valid and know that, to a greater or lesser extent, they're having a hard time.

You cannot 'fix' anyone's loneliness on your own, but your concern, kindness, and support can make a big difference. For a start, do tell the other person that you want to support them. Don't just assume that they know this; they might need you to say it.

Let them know when you are available; say, for example, 'I'm always around to chat at the weekend/in the evenings/on a Tuesday and Thursday morning.' Knowing that someone is just a phone call away can be reassuring and comforting to someone who is lonely.

Call, visit, email, or message them regularly to keep in touch. That might be every few days, once a week, or once every two weeks – whatever is appropriate. Sometimes leave a voicemail message just to say hello and that you were thinking of them, or a small piece of news or something amusing you know they'd like to hear. Knowing that someone else is keeping them in mind can, in itself, give someone a sense of connection.

Help Someone to Be More Connected

Being supportive with someone who is lonely involves getting the right balance; understanding and accepting how the other person is feeling but without getting completely caught up in their situation and feeling solely responsible for easing their loneliness.

Aim to help them take the focus off their feelings of loneliness and isolation and instead focus on what they can do. Talk with the other person about what they want and need. Do they want to get to know more people – make friends and join in activities with other people? Perhaps they want someone – one or two people – in their lives that they can feel close to, share a warmth and understanding with? Perhaps they're experiencing a difficult time or have been through a trauma; they're struggling and need specialist and/or professional help?

Do be aware that a face-to-face conversation about their loneliness might feel uncomfortable. Simple activities done together like going for a walk, going for a drive, cooking together, or doing a household chore can be a good opportunity to talk about how they're feeling rather than a direct conversation.

Share Time and Activities Together

Every person's experience of loneliness may be different from someone else's and every person has different needs. It's not always easy to know exactly how to help.

An obvious place to start is to think of interesting, relaxing, and/or fun things you can do *together*.

Sometimes, if the other person isn't that talkative, rather than get together for a meal, do an activity together first to give you something to talk about over dinner.

Offer to accompany the other person to an appointment they may have – a medical or legal appointment, for example.

If you are part of a couple and the other person is on their own, invite the friend to join the two of you for a drink at the pub, breakfast at a cafe, lunch or dinner. Maybe they'd like to join you for a walk, or a shopping trip to Ikea. A relative of mine told me that in her post-divorce despair, some of her most relaxed, enjoyable times were when her friend and partner just invited her to come over, plop down on the sofa, have a drink, and stay for dinner.

Inviting them along to a social gathering – a club or a party – in order to get them out and meeting new people is a good idea but don't abandon them. Throwing your friend into a social situation while you happily chat to others is almost guaranteed to leave them feeling worse than before. If you invite someone to a social gathering, it's still your responsibility to make sure they feel comfortable and secure. Introduce them to others and include them in conversations. If, for example you were including your friend Joe in a conversation with others, you might ask, 'What do you think about that Joe?' Or 'That happened to you, Joe, didn't it?' and wait for them to join in.

Invites to weekends away, to events, gigs, shows, and exhibitions are all good but often, regular small gestures – as opposed to an overly generous invitation that can leave the other person feeling that you're just inviting them because you pity them or feel sorry for them – are often just as much appreciated.

Whatever you do, be reliable. Try not to reschedule plans or cancel at the last minute. Forgetting a promised phone call or a cancelled outing can be a big disappointment for someone with little contact with others.

If you have other commitments or live far away and so can't meet up with the other person very often, see if anyone else – a friend, relative, neighbour, or volunteer from a relevant support organization – can help you to make sure that the person sees or speaks to someone regularly.

Connecting with Other People

Talk with the other person about what sort of social activities they like. Do they want to join in with something with a group of others or just one or two people? Do they want to get involved in activities on a weekly basis?

Find out what's important to them, what they'd like in the way of social contact. Then, talk together about their answers to the following questions and issues:

- Who do they already know and spend time with?
- What do they already do, what do they already know, and what resources do they currently have to help alleviate their loneliness? Do they need access to transport, for example, to get them to social activities?
- What further information, resources, or help will they need?
- What might the options and opportunities be?
- What are their concerns about connecting with other people? Are they, for example, not feeling confident about connecting with other people?

Help the other person to research what activities, services, support, and information are available for them; help them to find out about Meetup groups, classes and courses, and/or voluntary work that may be of interest.

Encourage the other person to commit to specific actions – one step at a time – so that they can help themselves and move forward. Once they've identified something to aim for – perhaps to join a new activity or invite someone to do something with them – do be positive and encouraging.

If they're resistant, find out what, exactly, their concerns are. Encouraging someone doesn't mean you deny the difficulties. Instead, acknowledge the challenges and then point out what qualities, strengths, and resources they have that will help them to take steps to connect with others and be less lonely. Remind them of their reason to connect with other people; what they'll gain, how they'll improve their situation.

They may need some support to make new social connections or access services designed to connect people and reduce loneliness. Going to things alone – especially for the first time – is not easy. You could go to something with them for the first time.

My parents used to do a lot of walking in the country before my dad died. Mum had heard about a local walking group but was apprehensive about going along. I went with her to the first couple of group walks and after that she was quite happy to go along without me. And because I'd met members of the walking group, I knew who she meant when she was telling me anything about them.

So, if they find the idea of going somewhere new, on their own, daunting, do suggest you come with them to the first meeting or event. Of course, that's not so likely if you're the parent of a teenager! In that case, suggest they ask another family member or someone else they know to go with them.

Setting Limits

Ellie's mother Doreen belongs to a social club that meets once a week. Doreen has recently been diagnosed with cataracts and has been told not to drive until after an operation to remove them. The operation will be some months from now. She tells Ellie she still wants to go to the club but doesn't want to get the bus there and back. Doreen asks Ellie if *she* will take her each week. Ellie says she does not want to commit to taking her mum to the club and back each week and suggests Doreen phones another club member for a lift.

Doreen says she's anxious about asking someone else for a lift in case they say no and then Doreen would feel embarrassed. From past experience, Ellie knows if she says she'll give her mum a lift this time, Doreen will find other situations when she needs Ellie to be her taxi service. Instead, Ellie suggests that she either gets the bus to the club and back with Doreen next week so that Doreen can get the bus on her own in future, or she gives her mum a lift to the club next week, and together, they could find out if there was someone else in the group who could give Doreen a lift each week.

In order to build confidence, it's important to give a person time to help them overcome challenges gradually. Don't push them into situations that, for one reason or another, are too much to handle. Let the person decide how much or how little they feel comfortable with, but always encourage them to move forward. Reassure them that it can take time and effort and that they shouldn't be disheartened if things aren't moving at the pace they'd like them to.

Supporting Someone Experiencing Emotional or Existential Loneliness

When it comes to supporting people who are lonely, so often, the focus is on creating opportunities for them to connect with other people. An important point to remember about loneliness is that it's not always about a lack of people in a person's life; they may feel lonely because of a lack of meaningful connections with others who they feel understand them and who they feel close to.

Certainly, joining in with others who have similar interests makes it more likely that a person will meet like-minded individuals with whom they can develop closer friendships.

But if the person you're concerned about – friend, colleague, partner, son, daughter, or other family member – has a particular difficulty, an issue that's contributing to their loneliness – a physical or mental health issue, for example, or a bereavement – they might feel no one really understands.

It can be difficult to know what, if anything, you can do to help. Often, it just means being physically there. You can also offer support by sharing in life's ordinary things, like walking, cooking, or simply sitting together in silence. If you live far away, it's just keeping contact and letting them know you're at the end of the phone if they need to talk. A text or a call to let them know you're thinking of them can go a long way.

You might worry about saying the wrong thing – perhaps you're worried that mentioning what happened will stir up upsetting emotions and so you say nothing. Simply ask 'How are you today?' or 'How have you been this last week?' They might not want to say much, And that's OK. By asking, you show that you aren't afraid to acknowledge their grief or trauma. But if they do open up, you do need to feel comfortable enough to listen to whatever the person wants to say.

And that may be all you have to do: listen to what they're saying and feeling. Don't interrupt, don't try to fix it, pacify them, offer solutions, or stop their experience or expression of what they're thinking or feeling. You don't need to say anything, just having someone who is willing to listen can help a person feel less alone and isolated.

Don't assume the other person will want to talk to you though. It can take time for them to feel able to talk openly. Putting pressure on them to talk might dissuade them from saying anything at all. Give them the time and space. When people are unhappy, being around them isn't easy, so in giving them space, you give yourself space as well.

Thoughtful Gesture

My friend Chris kept the last birthday card her mum gave her dad, Stan, before she died. Each birthday, Chris gets out the card from her mum and gives it to Stan. It's a lovely way to keep a connection!

Sometimes solutions are unnecessary, so don't feel you have to provide one. You may feel powerless about not being able to offer some practical help, but if you do feel it's appropriate, you can ask – 'Can I tell you what I know/who I know who has been through a similar experience?' or 'Would you like some advice? Or 'I have a couple of ideas for something I could do that might help. Would you like to hear them?'

There's lots of information and advice to be had from relevant support groups and charities. You may want to find out about helplines, forums, and support groups or professional help that's available and just give them the contact details.

Top Tip

Learn Something About What the Other Person Is Struggling With

The mental health charity Mind, for example, offers information and advice to people with mental health problems. They also recognize the challenges of supporting someone you love who is mentally ill. Their information and support page www.mind .org.uk/information-support/ explains how to cope when supporting someone else and gives practical suggestions for what *you* can do and where to go for help and support.

Reducing Loneliness at Work

People who are lonely at work are unhappy, and when people are unhappy at work it can have a detrimental impact on their ability to work well.

A person doesn't have to be working from home to feel lonely. Poor workplace conditions, disruptive shift patterns, and difficult team dynamics can affect anyone, regardless of their role.

How do you know if any of your employees or team are feeling lonely, cut off, and isolated? You ask them. And you ask what they think would help them feel more connected. Then you do what you can to help them feel included and connected – more involved and that they belong.

The UK Health and Safety Executive (HSE) has a survey template you can use to gather information from your staff about their wellbeing. You can find this on their website. Go to hse.gov.uk/ and put Indicator Tool into the search bar, then click on 'Work Related Stress Tools and Templates'. The survey template has questions (based on the HSE Management Standards) about mental wellbeing at work that, in addition to helping find out how people feel about their job, aims to identify issues around relationships at work, satisfaction with communication in the workplace, and how supported they feel.

Aim to Be Inclusive and to Develop a Culture of Connection and Community at Work

Aim to make your workplace a mutually supportive environment where people enjoy good work relationships. Think about introducing, for example, mentoring and buddying schemes to help new employees settle in quickly and feel part of things, and to promote positive working relationships.

The smallest gestures on your part, like making someone a coffee, saying 'hello' in the morning and goodbye at the end of the day go a long way to making a person feel included. So can asking if they have plans for the weekend, how they're feeling if they've been unwell or suffered a bereavement recently. Small kindnesses like these can make all the difference to how included people feel.

Developing a culture of care, interest, and inclusivity will likely help people feel safe and secure, which can give them the confidence to open up about their vulnerabilities. Do lead the way by not being afraid to talk openly and honestly (and appropriately – don't overshare!) about yourself and your own feelings. Rather than feel isolated and alone in any struggle they might be having – whether with a work or emotional issue – your being open helps others to know that they're not alone, that it's OK to say they're struggling and need help.

You can't force people to become friends at work. But you can encourage them to form bonds, by organizing inclusive social activities that bring people together. Here are some ideas:

- Use health-related activities for team building that boost both physical health and mental wellbeing, for example, charity fundraisers involving physical activities, shared 'healthy' lunches, a lunchtime walking or running club.
- Designate an area for lunchtime board games such as chess, Scrabble, checkers, mah-jongg, Risk, backgammon, and battleships.
- Organize a weekend or evening walk which includes bringing your dog, children, parents, or partner.

- Organize evening get-togethers that involve activities such as dancing or bowling, rather than just drinking.
- Get together for a good cause; organize volunteer days. Volunteering gives workers an opportunity to create and strengthen bonds while making a contribution to their community. Go to do-it.org/news/using-your-work-volunteer-days/ for information and ideas.

Whatever the activities, aim to be inclusive. Employees should not be or feel excluded because of their level of physical ability, cultural or religious beliefs, race, sexuality, ability, age or gender.

Finally, do keep a lookout for behaviour that separates and distances people from each other; people being inadvertently excluded, for example. Be aware of behaviour that alienates people from each other – bullying or harassment – and make it your mission to get the information and support you might need to deal with these effectively.

Volunteer

If you would like to become involved with the wider community in helping others to feel less lonely, there's a range of initiatives and organizations you can sign up to. Here are just three that need volunteers to chat and/or support others in your community to feel more connected and less lonely.

The WRVS's Community Companions service is an easy way for you to simply be there for someone. You can help people feel confident and remain independent by keeping them connected with others. www.volunteering .royalvoluntaryservice.org.uk/

Age UK offer free telephone friendship services which are staffed by volunteers. Many local Age UKs also offer face-to-face befriending. As a volunteer, you would visiting an older person in their home, perhaps for a cup of tea and a chat, or accompanying them to an activity (such as a trip to a cafe or the theatre). Age UK: www .ageuk.org.uk/ Silverline: www.thesilverline.org.uk/

The Chatty Café Scheme; as a Chatty Café ambassador at a Chatty Café venue. you'll meet new people and help strengthen connections within your community. Their website says: 'Volunteer with us and get back a whole lot more than you give'. https://thechattycafescheme.com/ uk/

There are many advice and support organizations that require volunteers for their helplines. All will offer training and support. Just get in touch with an organization and ask about voluntary opportunities.

In a nutshell

- Enable people to feel they belong, right from the start; be welcoming, approachable, and inclusive.

- If you know someone who is feeling lonely, do recognize feelings and emotions as valid and know that, to a greater or lesser extent, they're having a hard time.
- Your concern, kindness, and support can make a big difference. Don't just assume that they know you want to support them; they might need you to say it.
- Being supportive involves getting the right balance; understanding and accepting how the other person is feeling but without getting too caught up in their situation and feeling solely responsible for easing their loneliness.
- Think of interesting, relaxing, and/or fun things you can do together. Offer to accompany the other person to appointments they may have.
- Talk with the other person about what they want and need in terms social contact with others and what sort of social activities they might like to join in with.
- Help them to research what activities – Meetup groups, classes and courses, and/or voluntary opportunities – are available. Also, help find out what services, support, and information are available.
- Encourage the other person to commit to specific actions – one step at a time – so that they can help themselves and move forward. Once they've identified something to aim for, do be positive and encouraging.

- Don't push them into situations that may be too much to handle. Let the person decide how much or how little they feel comfortable with, but always encourage them to move forward.
- If they're resistant, find out what their concerns are. Acknowledge – don't dismiss – the challenges but remind them of their reason to connect with other people; what they'll gain, how they'll improve their situation.
- Going to things alone – especially for the first time – is not easy. You, another friend, or family member could go to something with them for the first time.
- Reassure them that it can take time and effort to feel less lonely and that they shouldn't be disheartened if things aren't moving at the pace they'd like them to.
- If the person you're concerned about has a particular difficulty or has experienced a trauma, it can be difficult to know what, if anything, you can do to help. Often, it just means being physically there.
- You might worry about saying the wrong thing and so say nothing. Just ask 'How are you today?' or 'How have you been this last week?'
- They might not want to say much. But if they do open up, you do need to feel comfortable enough to listen to whatever the person wants to say.
- If you have suggestions or advice, do ask first if they'd like to hear it. Find out about relevant

helplines, forums, and support groups or professional help that are available for the person you're concerned about.

- If you are an employer, manager, or supervisor, aim to be inclusive and to develop a culture of connection and community at work; a mutually supportive environment where people enjoy good working relationships.
- Find out if any of your employees or team are feeling lonely – cut off and isolated – by asking them. Ask what they think would help them feel more connected. Then do what you can to help them feel included, more involved, and that they belong.
- You can't force people at work to become friends. But you can encourage them to form bonds, by organizing inclusive social activities that bring people together.
- Be aware of behaviour that alienates people from each other – bullying or harassment – and make it your mission to get the information and support you might need to deal with these effectively.
- If you would like to become involved with the wider community in helping others to feel less lonely, there's a range of initiatives and organizations you can sign up to. All will offer training and support. Just get in touch with an organization and ask about voluntary opportunities.

Further Information and Support

Information and Research

Campaign to End Loncliness campaigntoendloneliness
.org.uk/ draws on research and inspiration from across
the country to offer information and ideas to both
individuals and those working with older people. They
deliver projects and campaigns with a range of other
organizations.

Let's talk Loneliness https://letstalkloneliness.co.uk/sup
port/ This website brings together organizations, resources, and inspirational stories that are united in a
shared aim: to get more people talking about loneliness.

The Loneliness Lab www.lonelinesslab.org/ Their aim
is to reduce loneliness in cities and urban environments
globally.

Jo Cox Foundation www.jocoxfoundation.org/loneliness
_commission/

In 2017, having talked with a wide range of people
who had experienced loneliness, the Jo Cox Loneliness

Commission published their report *Combating Loneliness One Conversation at a Time*.

Helplines and Support

The Silver Line www.thesilverline.org.uk/ is a free confidential helpline providing information, friendship, and advice to older people, open 24 hours a day, every day of the year on 0800 4 70 80 90. Their free Telephone Friendship Service matches people aged 60 and over with a friendly volunteer for a weekly chat.

Side by Side https://sidebyside.mind.org.uk/ is Mind's safe, moderated community where you can share your experiences of feeling lonely, anxious, depressed, and/or mental health problems.

Marmalade Trust www.marmaladetrust.org/ dedicated to raising awareness of loneliness and helping people make new friendships.

The Mix www.themix.org.uk/ The Mix is for young people under the age of 25. It provides information and support you might need to take on any challenge you're facing, from homelessness to finding a job, from money to mental health, from break-ups to drugs.

Social Groups

Meetup www.meetup.com/ enables people to find and join groups of other people in their local area who share each other's interests. There are Meetup groups to fit a wide range of interests, hobbies and identities, plus others you'll never have thought of.

Men's Sheds https://menssheds.org.uk/ are community spaces for men to connect, converse, and create.

The Women's Institute www.thewi.org.uk/, **The Townswomen's Guild** www.the-tg.com/, and **National Women's Register** www.nwr.org.uk/ are all community-based organizations for women that offer a wide range of activities and interest-based events.

National Council for the Divorced and Separated (Phoenix) https://ncdsw.org.uk/ recognize that you may not be looking for a relationship, but you don't know anyone else who is single to go to social events with. They provide a safe environment for you to go out and socialize with others and make new friends. If you would like to go to one of their clubs but do not want to attend alone, contact them and they'll arrange for one of their members to meet you outside the venue. (How thoughtful is that?!)

Classes and Courses

Find Courses www.findcourses.co.uk/search/fun-hobby-and-exercise-classes/ enables you to find leisure courses in your local area You can also search for courses at your local council's website. Put 'adult education' or 'adult learning' in the search bar.

The WEA www.wea.org.uk/ have courses and classes in almost every area of England and Scotland.

U3A u3a.org.uk/ has over 1000 locally run interest groups in the UK that provide a wide range of opportunities for older people to come together and learn and explore new ideas, skills, and activities.

Free Virtual Classes and Courses

Open University (OU) www.open.ac.uk/ offers more than degrees. They also have a wide range of free courses www.open.edu/openlearn/free-courses/full-catalogue/.

FutureLearn www.futurelearn.com/ allows you to learn online with world-class universities and industry experts. A wide range of FutureLearn's courses are free.

Duolingo www.duolingo.com/ Arabic, French, Spanish, and Welsh are just a few of more than 30 language courses that you can learn for free with Duolingo.

Websites and Apps to Connect with Others

Friender https://frienderapp.com/ is an app that connects people with common interests.

TogetherFriends www.togetherfriends.com/ is a friendship website just for women in the UK.

Peanut www.peanut-app.io/ is an app for mums to meet other mums.

Meet My Dog https://meetmydogapp.com/ is an app for dogs and their owners to meet each other's dogs and their owners.

Nextdoor https://nextdoor.co.uk/ connects neighbours to each other and to everything nearby.

The Chatty Café Scheme https://thechattycafescheme .co/uk/ encourages cafés and other venues such as pubs, libraries, and community centres to designate a Chatter & Natter table. This is where customers can sit if they are happy to talk to other customers. When you put in your location, Google will search for venues near you.

DialUp https://dialup.com/ Dialup will ring your phone and another Dialup member's phone on an automated schedule and pair you randomly in a one-on-one conversation.

Volunteering Opportunities

Spending some time doing something for someone else will not only give you something to do, it will also give you a real sense of purpose and connection.

The **Do It** website www.do-it.org/ allows you to search for all kinds of volunteering opportunities in the UK by entering your postcode or town.

You can also find out about volunteering opportunities near to you by contacting your local volunteer centre or visiting www.volunteering.org.uk/ and www.ncvo.org .uk/.

Below are examples of the thousands of volunteering opportunities in the UK:

Environmental Volunteering

The Conservation Volunteers www.tcv.org.uk/ and **The Wildlife Trusts** www.wildlifetrusts.org/ run outdoor volunteering projects around the UK. So do the **Woodland Trust** www.woodlandtrust.org.uk/, the **Marine Conservation Society** www.mcsuk.org/, and the **National Trust** www.nationaltrust.org.uk/.

Social Farms & Gardens www.farmgarden.org.uk/ have details of community garden and farms around the UK.

If you have a disability and want to start or continue gardening, **Thrive** www.thrive.org.uk/ can help.

The Good Gym www.goodgym.org./ run groups that combine getting fit with doing good.

Volunteer Work with Animals

Blue Cross www.bluecross.org.uk/volunteer/

The People's Dispensary for Sick Animals (PDSA) www .pdsa.org.uk/

The Royal Society for the Prevention of Cruelty to Animals (RSPCA) www.rspca.org.uk/

Volunteering in Sports

Join In www.doit.life/join-in/

Sport England www.sportengland.org/

Medical Volunteering

St John Ambulance www.sja.org.uk/

Red Cross www.redcross.org.uk/

Festival Medical Services www.festival-medical.org/get-involved/

Volunteering from Home

Missing Maps www.missingmaps.org/ Map a disaster zone.

Bag Books www.bagbooks.org/ Knit or sew a book bag for children.

Book mark www.bookmarkreading.org/ Help a child to read.

Project Implicit https://implicit.harvard.edu/implicit/aboutus.html/ Help researchers better understand society's hidden biases and prejudices and how we might tackle them.

AXS Map www.axsmap.com/ Help make shops and restaurants more accessible for people with disabilities.

Be My Eyes www.bemyeyes.com/ Help a blind or low-vision person to go about their daily tasks.

eBird https://ebird.org/home/ Track your bird sightings via the eBird website.

Amnesty Decoder https://decoders.amnesty.org/ Help Amnesty researchers sift through pictures, information, and documents and help expose human rights violations.

Help and Support for Specific Issues: Organizations and Support Groups

Bereavement

CRUSE www.cruse.org.uk/ provides support and information for people who have experienced bereavement.

The Way Foundation. https://widowedandyoung.org.uk/ provides emotional and practical support to young widowed men and women under the age of 50.

Just 'B' https://justb.org.uk/ offer emotional wellbeing, bereavement, and trauma support nationally to NHS, care sector staff, and emergency service workers.

The Good Grief Project www.thegoodgriefproject.co .uk/ supports families grieving after the untimely death of a loved one, particularly the death of a child.

Child Bereavement UK www.childbereavementuk.org/ helps children and young people (up to age 25), parents, and families to rebuild their lives when a child grieves or when a child dies.

Tommy's www.tommys.org/ provide support for people who have experienced pregnancy loss.

Victim of a Crime

Victim Support www.victimsupport.org.uk/ provides specialist practical and emotional support to victims and witnesses of crime.

Rape Crisis Their website https://rapecrisis.org.uk/ provides a range of services for women and girls who have experienced abuse, domestic violence, and sexual assault. Over half their member Rape Crisis Centres provide specific support services for men and boys too.

Being Stalked www.suzylamplugh.org/Pages/Category/ national-stalking-helpline/ Suzy Lamplugh Trust understand that it can feel difficult seeking support. But they *can* help.

Domestic Abuse www.nationaldahelpline.org.uk/ and **Women's Aid** www.womensaid.org.uk/ are two organizations that can help.

Whistleblowing www.protect-advice.org.uk/ If you've seen, heard, or suspect wrongdoing in your workplace, or know of a serious risk or accident 'waiting to happen' **Protect** can advise you.

Bullying and Harassment at Work

ACAS www.acas.org.uk/ have a helpline that can provide you with impartial advice on what to do if you're being bullied at work.

Citizens Advice www.citizensadvice.org.uk/ can also provide information and advice.

Dating and Romance Scams www.moneyadviceservice .org.uk/blog/how-to-spot-and-avoid-dating-scams/ has advice on how to spot and avoid online dating scams and where to go for help if you have been a victim.

Support for Specific Issues and Challenges

Debt www.moneyadviceservice.org.uk/ The **Money Advice Service** say that they can point you in the direction of free advice services available across the UK. Go to their website and search for 'Debt Advice'.

Carers UK www.carersuk.org/ are there to listen, to give you expert information and advice that's tailored to your situation, to champion your rights, and support you in finding new ways to manage at home, at work, or wherever you are.

Young carers Both **Spurgeons Children's Charity** https://spurgeons.org/ and Barnardo's www.barnardos.org.uk/ offer a wide range of services to support young carers.

Insomnia www.sleepwithmepodcast.com/ lulls listeners to sleep with bedtime stories.

Feeling Suicidal

Samaritans www.samaritans.org/ You can call their phone number, 116 123, or email jo@samaritans.org If you're feeling suicidal, please don't struggle on your own. Do call or email them.

Get Out in Nature

The Wildlife Trusts (www.wildlifetrusts.org/) have a searchable online map of its nature reserves, almost all of which have free entry; it also provides a list of accessible nature reserves. And Ordnance Survey's Greenspace getoutside.ordnancesurvey.co.uk/greenspaces/ shows thousands of green spaces for leisure and recreation.

BorrowMyDoggy borrowmydoggy.com/ connects dog owners with others who would like to walk or dog-sit and share the care of a dog.

Counselling and Therapy

These websites all have details of qualified registered therapists:

- The UK Council for Psychotherapy (UKCP) https://psychotherapy.org.uk/
- The British Association of Counselling and Psycho-therapy (BACP) www.bacp.co.uk/
- Welldoing https://welldoing.org/

Podcast

Alonement: How To Be Alone and Absolutely Own It www.alonement.com/alonement-podcast/ Francesca Specter interviews people about the positive aspects of spending time alone.

Books by Gill Hasson

Mindfulness. Be Mindful. Live in the Moment.

Mindfulness Pocketbook: Little Exercises for a Calmer Life

Confidence Pocketbook: Little Exercises for a Self-Assured Life

Positive Thinking: Find Happiness and Achieve Your Goals Through the Power of Positive Thought

Positive Thinking Pocketbook: Little Exercises for a Happy and Successful Life

The Self-Care Handbook: Connect with Yourself and Boost Your Wellbeing

Overcoming Anxiety: Reassuring Ways to Break Free from Stress and Worry and Lead a Calmer Life

Kindness: Change Your Life and Make the World a Kinder Place

Emotional Intelligence: Managing Emotions to Make a Positive Impact on Your Life and Career

Mental Health and Wellbeing in the Workplace: A Practical Guide for Employers and Employees

Happiness: How to Get Into the Habit of Being Happy

About the Author

Gill Hasson has written more than 25 books on the subject of wellbeing for adults and children: books on emotional intelligence, resilience, mindfulness, overcoming anxiety, happiness, and kindness. She also delivers teaching and training for education organizations, voluntary and business organizations, and the public sector.

Gill's particular interest and motivation is in helping people to realize their potential and to live their best life! You can contact Gill at gillhasson@btinternet.com

Index